David Starr Jordan

The Care and Culture of Men

A Series of Addresses on the Higher Education

David Starr Jordan

The Care and Culture of Men
A Series of Addresses on the Higher Education

ISBN/EAN: 9783337407964

Printed in Europe, USA, Canada, Australia, Japan

Cover: Foto ©Suzi / pixelio.de

More available books at **www.hansebooks.com**

THE CARE AND CULTURE
OF MEN

A SERIES OF ADDRESSES

ON THE

HIGHER EDUCATION

BY

DAVID STARR JORDAN

PRESIDENT OF LELAND STANFORD JUNIOR UNIVERSITY
AND OF THE CALIFORNIA ACADEMY OF SCIENCES

" The best Political Economy is the care and culture of men."
—EMERSON.

SAN FRANCISCO
THE WHITAKER & RAY COMPANY
(INCORPORATED)
1896

TO
JANE LATHROP STANFORD

PREFATORY NOTE.

THIS volume is made up of addresses relating to higher education, delivered at different times before assemblies of teachers and students. The writer is under obligation to the publishers of the Popular Science Monthly, the Forum, and the Occidental Medical Times for the permission to reprint articles which have appeared in these periodicals. The article on "The Evolution of the College Curriculum," first published in "Science Sketches," is here reprinted by consent of A. C. McClurg & Co., and that on "The Higher Education of Women" is reprinted by consent of the Irving Syndicate. Most of the articles have been freely retouched since their original publication.

PALO ALTO, CAL., May 14, 1896.

TABLE OF CONTENTS.

THE CARE AND CULTURE OF MEN.

I.

THE VALUE OF HIGHER EDUCATION.

WHAT I have to say here is addressed to young men and young women. It is a plea, as strong as I know how to make it, for higher education, for more thorough preparation for the duties of life. I know those well to whom I wish to speak. And to such as these, with the life and duties in the busy world before you, the best advice I or any one can give is this: "Go to college."

And you may say: "These four years are among the best of my life. The good the college does must be great, if I should spend this time and money in securing it. What will the college do for me?"

It may do many things for you,— if you are made of the right stuff; for you cannot fasten a two-thousand-dollar education to a fifty-cent boy. The fool, the dude, and the shirk come out of college pretty much as they went in. They dive deep in the Pierian springs, as the duck dives in the pond,— and they come up as dry as the duck does. The college will not do everything for

---

*Address before the California State Teachers' Association at Fresno, 1892.

you. It is simply one of the helps by which you can win your way to a noble manhood or womanhood. Whatever you are, you must make of yourself; but a well-spent college life is one of the greatest helps to all good things.

So, if you learn to use it rightly, this the college can do for you: It will bring you in contact with the great minds of the past, the long roll of those who, through the ages, have borne a mission to young men and young women, from Plato to Emerson, from Homer and Euripides to Schiller and Browning. Your thought will be limited not by the narrow gossip of to-day, but the great men of all ages and all climes will become your brothers. You will learn to feel what the Greek called the "consolations of philosophy." To turn from the petty troubles of the day to the thoughts of the masters, is to go from the noise of the street through the door of a cathedral. If you learn to unlock these portals, no power on earth can take from you the key. The whole of your life must be spent in your own company, and only the educated man is good company for himself. The uneducated man looks out on life through narrow windows, and thinks the world is small.

The college can bring you face to face with the great problems of nature. You will learn from your study of nature's laws more than the books can tell you of the grandeur, the power, the omnipotence of God. You will learn to face great problems seriously. You will learn to work patiently at their solution, though you know that many generations must each add its mite to your work before any answer can be reached.

Your college course will bring you in contact with

men whose influence will strengthen and inspire. The
ideal college professor should be the best man in the
community. He should have about him nothing mean,
or paltry, or cheap. He should be to the student as
David Copperfield's Agnes, "always pointing the way
upward."

That we are all this, I shall not pretend. Most college professors whom I know are extremely human.
We have been soured, and starved, and dwarfed in many
ways, and many of us are not the men we might have
been if we had had your chances for early education.
But unpractical, pedantic, fossilized though the college
professor may be, his heart is in the right place ; he is
not mercenary, and his ideals are those of culture and
progress. We are keeping the torch burning which you,
young men of the twentieth century, may carry to the
top of the mountain.

But here and there among us is the ideal teacher,
the teacher of the future, the teacher to have known
whom is of itself a liberal education. I have met some
such in my day — Louis Agassiz, Charles Frederick
Hartt, Asa Gray, George William Curtis, James Rus-
sell Lowell, Andrew Dickson White, among others, and
there are many more such in our land. It is worth ten
years of your life to know well one such man as these.
Garfield once said that a log with Mark Hopkins at one
end of it and himself at the other, would be a university.
In whatever college you go, poor and feeble though
the institution may be, you will find some man who, in
some degree, will be to you what Mark Hopkins was
to Garfield. To know him will repay you for all your
sacrifices. It was said of Dr. Nott, of Union College,

that he "took the sweepings of other colleges, and sent them back into society pure gold." Such was his influence on young men.

Moreover, the training which comes from association with one's fellow-students cannot be overestimated. Here and there, it is true, some young invertebrate, overburdened with money or spoiled by home-coddling, falls into bad company, and leaves college in worse condition than when he entered it. These are the windfalls of education. However much we may regret them, we cannot prevent their existence. But they are few among the great majority. Most of our apples are not worm-eaten at the core. The average student enters college for a purpose ; and you will lose nothing, but may gain much, from association with him. Among our college students are the best young men of the times. They mold each other's character, and shape each other's work. Many a college man will tell you that, above all else which the college gave, he values the friendships which he formed in school. In the German universities, the "fellow-feeling among free spirits" is held to be one of the most important elements in their grand system of higher education.

Many a great genius has risen and developed in solitude, as the trailing arbutus grows in the woods and scorns cultivation. Poets sing because their souls are full of music, not because they have learned the gamut of passions in schools. But all great work, in science, in philosophy, in the humanities, has come from entering into the work of others.

There was once a Chinese emperor who decreed that he was to be the first; that all history was to begin with him, and that nothing should be before him. But we cannot enforce such decree. We are not emperors of China. The world's work, the world's experience does not begin with us. We must know what has been done before. We must know the paths our predecessors have trodden, if we would tread them farther. We must stand upon their shoulders — dwarfs upon the shoulders of the giants — if we would look farther into the future than they. Science, philosophy, statesmanship cannot for a moment let go of the past.

The college intensifies the individuality of a man. It takes his best abilities and raises him to the second, or third, or tenth power, as we say in algebra. It is true enough that colleges have tried, and some of them still try, to enforce uniformity in study — to cast all students in the same mold. Colleges have been conservative, old-fogyish, if you please. Musty old men in the dust of libraries have tried to make young men dry and dreary like themselves. Colleges have placed readiness above thoroughness, memory above mastery, glibness above sincerity, uniformity above originality, and the dialectics of the dead past above the work of the living present. The scepter of the Roman emperor has crumbled into dust, but the "rod of the Roman schoolmaster is over us still."

But say what you will of old methods, they often attained great ends. Colleges have aimed at uniformity. They did not secure it. The individuality of the student bursts through the cast-iron curriculum. "The man's the man for a' that," and the man is so much more the man nature meant him to be, because his mind is trained.

The educated man has the courage of his convictions, because only he has any real convictions. He knows how convictions should be formed. What he believes he takes on his own evidence — not because it is the creed of his church or the platform of his party. So he counts as a unit in his community — not as part of a dozen or a hundred whose opinions are formed by their town's place on the map, or who train under the party flag because their grandfathers did the same. "To see things as they really are," is one of the crowning privileges of the educated man, and to help others to see them so, is one of the greatest services he can render to the community.

But you may say: "All this may be fine and true, but it does not apply in my case. I am no genius; I shall never be a scholar. I want simply to get along. Give me education enough to teach a district school, or to run an engine, or to keep account-books, and I am satisfied. Any kind of a school will be good enough for that."

"The youth gets together his materials," says Thoreau, "to build a bridge to the moon, or perchance a palace or temple on the earth, and, at length, the middle-aged man concludes to build a woodshed with them."

Now, why not plan for a woodshed at first, and save this waste of time and materials?

But this is the very good of it. The gathering of these materials will strengthen the youth. It may be the means of saving him from idleness, from vice. So long as you are at work on your bridge to the moon, you will shun the saloon, and we shall not see you on the dry-goods box in front of the corner-grocery. I know many a man who in early life planned only to build a woodshed, but who found later that he had the strength to build a temple, if he only had the materials. Many a man the world calls successful would give all life has brought him could he make up for the disadvantages of his lack of early training. It does not hurt a young man to be ambitious in some honorable direction. In the pure-minded youth, ambition is the sum of all the virtues. Lack of ambition means failure from the start. The young man who is aiming at nothing, and cares not to rise, is already dead. There is no hope for him. Only the sexton and the undertaker can serve his purposes.

The old traveler, Rafinesque, tells us that, when he was a boy, he read the voyages of Captain Cook, and Pallas, and Le Vaillant, and his soul was fired with the desire to be a great traveler like them. "And so I became such," he adds shortly.

If you say to yourself, "I will be a naturalist, a traveler, an historian, a statesman, a scholar"; if you never unsay it; if you bend all your powers in that direction, and take advantage of all those aids that help toward your ends, and reject all that do not, you will some time reach your goal. *The world turns aside to let any man pass who knows whither he is going.*

"Why should we call ourselves men," said Mirabeau," unless it be to succeed in everything, everywhere? Say of nothing, 'This is beneath me,' nor feel that anything is beyond your powers. Nothing is impossible to the man who can will."

"But a college education costs money," you may say. "I have no money; therefore, I cannot go to college."

But this is nonsense. If you have health and strength, and no one dependent on you, you cannot be poor. There is, in this country, no greater good luck that a young man can have than to be thrown on his own resources. The cards are stocked against the rich man's son. Of the many college men who have risen to prominence in my day, very few did not lack for money in college. I remember a little boarding-club of the students at Cornell, truthfully called the "Struggle for Existence," and named for short, "The Strug," which has graduated more bright minds than any other single organization in my Alma Mater.

The young men who have fought their way, have earned their own money, and know what a dollar costs, have the advantage of the rich. They enter the world outside with no luxurious habits, with no taste for idleness. It is not worth while to be born with a silver spoon in your mouth, when a little effort will secure you a gold one. The time, the money that the unambitious young man wastes in trifling pursuits or in absolute idleness will suffice to give the ambitious man his education. The rich man's son may enter college with better preparation than you. He may wear better clothes. He may graduate younger. But the poor man's son can make up for lost time by greater energy and by the greater clearness of his grit. He steps from the commencement stage into no unknown world. He has already measured swords with the great antagonist, and the first victory is his. It is the first struggle that counts.

But it is not poverty that helps a man. There is no virtue in poor food or shabby clothing. It is the effort by which he throws off the yoke of poverty that enlarges the powers. It is not hard work, but work to a purpose, that frees the soul. If the poor man lie down in the furrow and say: "I won't try. I shall never amount to anything. I am too poor; and if I wait to earn money, I shall be too old to go to school." If you do this, I say, you won't amount to anything, and later in life you will be glad to spade the rich man's garden and to shovel his coal at a dollar a day.

I have heard of a poor man in Wisconsin who earns a half-dollar every day by driving a cow to pasture. He watches her all day as she eats, and then drives her home at night. This is all he does. Put here your half-dollar and there your man. The one balances the other, and the one enriches the world as much as the other. If it were not for the cow, the world would not need that man at all!

A young man can have no nobler ancestry than one made up of men and women who have worked for a living and who have given honest work. The instinct of industry runs in the blood. Naturalists tell us that the habits of one generation may be inherited by the next, reappearing as instincts. Whether this be literally true or not, this we know: it is easy to inherit laziness. No money or luck will place the lazy man on the level of his industrious neighbor. The industry engendered by the pioneer life of the last generation is still in your veins. Sons and daughters of the Western pioneers, yours is the best blood in the realm. You must make the most of yourselves. If you cannot get an education in four years, take ten years. It is worth your while. Your place in the world will wait for you till you are ready to fill it. Do not say that I am expecting too much of the effects of a firm resolution; that I give you advice which will lead you to failure. For the man who will fail will never make a resolution. Those among you whom fate has cut out for nobodies are the ones who will never try!

I said just now that you cannot put a two-thousand-dollar education on a fifty-cent boy. This has been tried again and again. It is tried in every college. It fails almost every time. What of that? It does not hurt to try. A few hundred dollars is not much to spend on an experiment like that; — the attempt to make a man out of a boy whose life might otherwise be a waste of so much good oxygen.

But what shall we say of a man who puts a fifty-cent education on a ten-thousand-dollar, a million-dollar boy, and narrows and cramps him throughout his after life? And just this is what ten thousand parents to-day in California are doing for their sons and daughters. Twenty years hence, ten thousand men and women of California will blame them for their shortness of sight and narrowness of judgment, in weighing a few paltry dollars, soon earned, soon lost, against the power which comes from mental training.

"For a man to have died who might have been wise and was not — this," says Carlyle, "I call a tragedy."

Another thing which should never be forgotten is this: A college education is not a scheme to enable a man to live without work. Its purpose is to help him to work to advantage — to make every stroke count. I have heard a father say sometimes: "I have worked hard all my life. I will give my boy an education, so that he will not have to drudge as I have had to do." And the boy going out in the world does not work as his father did. The result every time is disappointment; for the manhood which the son attains depends directly on his own hard work. But if the father says: "My son shall be a worker, too; but I will give him an education, so that his work may count for more to himself and to the world than my work has done for me." Then, if the son be as persistent as his father, the results of his work may be far beyond the expectations of either. The boys who are *sent* to college often do not amount to much. From the boys who *go* to college come the leaders of the future.

Frederic Denison Maurice tells us that "All experience is against the notion that the means to produce a supply of good, ordinary men is to attempt nothing higher. I know that nine-tenths of those the university sends out must be hewers of wood and drawers of water; but if I train the ten-tenths to be such, then the wood will be badly cut, and the water will be spilt. Aim at something noble. Make your system of education such that a great man may be formed by it, and there will be a manhood in your little men of which you did not dream!"

"You will hear every day around you," says Emerson, "the maxims of a low prudence. You will hear that your first duty is to get land and money, place and name. 'What is this truth you seek? What is this beauty?' men will ask in derision. If, nevertheless, God has called any of you to explore truth and beauty, be bold, be firm, be true! When you shall say, 'As others do, so will I. I renounce, I am sorry for it, my early visions. I must eat the good of the land and let learning and romantic expectations go until a more convenient season.'

Then dies the man in you. Then once more perish the buds of art, and poetry, and science, as they have died already in a hundred thousand men. The hour of that choice is the crisis of your destiny.''

But you may ask me this question : '' Will a college education pay, considered solely as a financial investment? ''

Again I must answer, ''Yes.'' But the scholar is seldom disposed to look upon his power as a financial investment. He can do better than to get rich. The scholar will say, as Agassiz said to the Boston publisher, ''I have no time, sir, to make money.''

But in the rank and file it is true that the educated men get the best salaries. In every field, from football to statesmanship, it is always science that wins the game. Brain-work is higher than hand-work, and it is worth more in any market. The man with the mind is the boss, and the boss receives a larger salary than the hands whose work he directs.

George William Curtis has said: ''I have heard it said that liberal education does not promote success in life. A chimney-sweep might say so. Without education he could gain the chimney-top — poor little blackamoor! — brandish his brush and sing his song of escape from soot to sunshine. But the ideal of success measures the worth of the remark that it may be attained without liberal education. If the accumulation of money be the standard, we must admit that a man might make a fortune in a hundred ways without education. But he could make a fortune, also, without purity of life, or noble character, or lofty faith. A man can pay much too high a price for money, and not every man who buys it knows its relative value with other possessions. Undoubtedly, Ezra Cornell and Matthew Vassar did not go to college, and they succeeded in life. But their success — what was it? Where do you see it now? Surely not in their riches, but in the respect that tenderly cherishes their memory, because, knowing its inestimable value, they gave to others the opportunity of education which had been denied to them."

Some time ago, Chancellor Lippincott, of the State University of Kansas, wrote to each of the graduates of that institution, asking them to state briefly the advantages which their experience showed that they have derived from their college life and work.

Among these answers, I may quote a few:

One says: "My love for the State grew with every lesson I received through her care. I saved five years of my life by her training, and I am a more loyal and a better citizen."

Another says this: "I have a better standing in the community than I could have gained in any other way."

Another says: "I would not exchange the advantages gained for a hundred times their cost, either to Kansas or to myself."

Another declares: "It is financially the best investment I ever made."

To another it had given "strong friendship with the most intelligent young men of the State, those who are certain to largely influence its destiny."

One said: "It has given me a place and an influence among a class of men whom I could not otherwise reach at all."

Another said: "I am better company for myself, and a better citizen, with far more practical interest in the State."

Thus it is in Kansas, and thus it is everywhere. To the young man or young woman of character, the college education does pay, from whatever standpoint you may choose to regard it.

When I was a boy on a farm in Western New York, some one urged my parents to send me to college. "But what will he find to do when he gets through college?" they asked. "Never mind that," a friend said; "he will always find plenty to do. There is always room at the top." There is always room at the top! All our professions are crowded in America, but the crowd is around the bottom of the ladder!

We are proud, and justly proud, of our common-school system. The free school stands on every Northern cross-road, and it is rapidly finding its way into the great New South. Every effort is made for the education of the masses. There is no upper caste to reap the benefits of an education, for which the poor man has to pay. There is no class educated and ruling by right of birth — no hereditary House of Lords. Our scholars and our leaders are of the people, from the people. The American plan is making us an intelligent people, as compared with the masses of any other nation. The number of those indifferent or ignorant is less in our Northern States than in England, or Germany, or France. But our leadership is worse than theirs. We have, for our numbers, fewer educated men than they have in any of these countries. Our statesmen are but children by the side of Gladstone or Bismarck. We are all too familiar with the American type of "statesman." The cross-ties of the railroads which lead in every direction out of Washington are every fourth year graven with the prints of his returning boot-heels. He is the butt of our national jokes, as well as the sign of our national shame! We have been too busy chopping our trees and breaking our prairies to educate our sons. Thus it comes, that in literature, in science, in philosophy, in everything except mechanical invention, American work has been contented to bear the stamp of mediocrity.

This is not so true as it was a few years ago; for Young America has made great strides toward the front in all these fields within the last twenty years. But it should not be true to any extent at all. Nowhere in the world, I believe, is the raw material out of which scholars and statesmen should be made so abundant as in America. Nowhere is native intelligence and energy so plentiful; but far too often does it waste itself in unworthy achievement. The journalist Sala says that "nowhere in the world is so much talent lying around loose as in America." In other words, in no other country are so many men of natural ability who fail in effectiveness in life for want of proper training.

In the different training-schools of California, large and small, nearly two thousand young people are gathered together to prepare for the profession of teaching. Of these, not one in fifty remains in school long enough to secure even the rudiments of a liberal education. Fifteen minutes for dinner; fifty weeks for an education! For the lowest grades of schools, there are candidates by the hundred; but when one of our really good schools wants a man for a man's work, it can make no use of these teachers.   We must search far and wide for the man to whom a present offer of fifty dollars a month has not seemed more important than all the grand opportunities the scholar may receive.   Many of our young teachers are making a mistake in this regard. Every year the demand for educated men and women in our profession is growing.   Every year scores of half-educated teachers are crowded out of their places to make way for younger men who have the training which the coming years demand.   What kind of a teacher do you mean to be?   One who has a basis of culture, and will grow as the years go on, or one with nothing in him, who will hang on, a burden to the profession, until he is finally turned out to starve?   What is the use of preparing for certain failure?   The bird in the hand is not worth ten in the bush.·   You cannot afford to sell your future at so heavy a discount.

The general purpose of public education, it is said, is the elevation of the masses.   This is well; but as the man is above the mass, there is a higher aim than this. Training of the individual is to break up the masses, to draw from the multitude the man.   We see a regiment of soldiers on parade — a thousand men; in dress and mein all are alike — the mass.   To the sound of the drum or the command of the officer, they move as one man. By and by, in the business of war, comes the cry for a man to lead some forlorn hope, to do some deed of bravery in the face of danger.   From the mass steps the man.   His training shows itself.   On parade, no more, no less than the others; he stands above them all on the day of trial.   So, too, in other things, in other places; for the need of men is not alone on the field of battle.

Some fifty thousand boys are to-day at play on the fields of California. Which of these shall be the great, the good of California's next century? Which of these shall redeem our State from its vassalage to the saloon and the spoilsman? Which of these shall be a center of sweetness and light; so that the world shall say, "It is good to have lived in California." Good not alone for the climate, the mountains, the forest, and the sea, the thousand beauties of nature which make our State so lovable; but good because life in California is life among the best and truest of men and women. This record California has yet to make; and there are some among you, I trust, who will live to help make it.

These fifty thousand boys form a part of what will be the masses. Let us train them as well as we can. Let us feed them well. Let us send them to school. Let us make them wise, intelligent, clean, honest, thrifty. Among them here and there is the future leader of men. Let us raise him from the masses, or, rather, let us give him a chance to raise himself; for the pine-tree in the thicket needs no outside help to place its head above the chaparral and sumac. To break up the masses, that they may be masses no more, but living men and women, is the mission of higher education.

In medicine, America is still the paradise of quacks. In law, the land is full of shysters and pettifoggers, and doers of "fine work"; but of good lawyers, the supply never equals the demand. In education, no land is so full as America of frauds and shams. The catalogues of our schools read like the advertisements of our patent medicines. They "cure all ills that flesh is heir to; one bottle sufficient!" The name "University" in America

c

is assumed by the cross-roads academy as well as by
Harvard or Johns Hopkins.   The name "Professor" is
applied to the country schoolmaster, the barber, and the
manager of the skating-rink.   The bachelor's diploma
in half our States is given by consent of law to those who
could not pass the examinations of any decent high
school.   Such diplomas do not ennoble their holders,
but they do serve to bring into contempt the very name
of American graduate.

One of the besetting sins of American life is its willingness to call very little things by very large names —
its tolerance of imposition and fraud.   It is the mission
of the scholar in each profession to combat fraud; to
show men "facts amid appearances"; to say that a pop-
gun is a pop-gun, though every one else may be calling
it a cannon!   As our country grows older, perhaps the
number of bladders will diminish.   If not, let us have
more pins!

What does the college do for the moral, the religious
training of the youth?   Let us examine.   If your
college assume to stand *in loco parentis*, with rod in
hand and spy-glasses on its nose, it will not do much
in the way of moral training.   The fear of punishment
will not make young men moral and religious; still less
a punishment so easily evaded as the discipline of the
college.

If your college claims to be a reform school, your professors detective officers, and your president a chief of
police, the students will give them plenty to do. . A college cannot take the place of the parent.   To claim that
it does so, is a mere pretense.   It can cure the boy of
petty vices and childish trickery only by making him a

man, by giving him higher ideals, more serious views
of life. You may win by inspiration, not by fear.

Take those dozen students, of whom Agassiz tells us
— his associates in the University of Munich. Do you
suppose that Dr. Döllinger caught any of them cheating
on examination? Did the three young men who knelt
under the haystack at Williamstown,— the founders of
our Foreign Missions,— choose the haystack rather than
the billiard-hall, for fear of the college faculty? "Free
should the scholar be, free and brave." "The petty
restraints that may aid in the control of college sneaks
and college snobs are an insult to college men and
women." And it is for the training of men and women
that the college exists.

So, too, in religious matters. The college can do
much, but not by rules and regulations. The college
will not make young men religious by enforced attendance at church or prayer-meeting. It will not awaken
the spiritual element in the student's nature by any system of demerit-marks. This the college can do for
religious culture: It can strengthen the student in his
search for truth. It can encourage manliness in him by
the putting away of childish things. Let the thoughts
of the student be as free as the air. Let him prove
all things, and he will hold fast to that which is good.
Give him a message to speak to other men, and when
he leaves your care you need fear for him, not the world,
the flesh, nor the Devil!

This is a practical age, we say, and we look askance at
dreams and ideals. We ask now: What is the value of
education? What is the value of Christianity? What is
the value of love, of God, of morality, of truth, of beau-

ty? — as though all these things were for sale in our city markets, somewhat shop-worn and going at a sacrifice.

"My son," says Victor Cherbuliez, "my son, we ought to lay up a stock of absurd enthusiasms in our youth, or else we shall reach the end of our journey with an empty heart; for we lose a great many of them by the way."

It is the noblest mission of all higher education, I believe, to fill the mind of the youth with these enthusiasms, with noble ideas of manhood, of work, of life. It should teach him to feel that life is indeed worth living; and no one who leads a worthy life has ever for a moment doubted this. It should help him to shape his own ambitions as to how a life may be made worthy. It should help him to believe that love, and friendship, and faith, and devotion are things that really exist, and are embodied in men and women. He should learn to know these men and women, whether of the present or of the past, and his life will become insensibly fashioned after theirs. He should form plans of his own work for society, for science, for art, for religion. His life may fall far short of what he would make it; but a high ideal must precede any worthy achievement.

A conviction or ideal in life must be a determination to work and live toward some end. It must express itself in action. It is destructive of mind and soul if an ideal stands in the place of effort. No visions and dreams uncontrolled by the will can be treated as independent sources of knowledge or power.

I once climbed a mountain slope in Utah, in midsummer, when every blade of grass was burned to a yellow crisp. I look over the valley, and here and there I can trace a line of vivid green across the fields, running down to the lake. I cannot see the water, but I know that the brook is there; for the grass would not grow without help. Like this brook in the hot plains, may be the life of the scholar in the world of men.

I look out over the struggling men and women. I see the weary soul, the lost ambitions,

> "The haggard face, the form that drooped and fainted
> In the fierce race for wealth."

Here and there I trace some line in life along which I see springing up all things good and gracious. Here is the scholar's work. In his pathway are all things beautiful and true — the love of nature, the love of man, the love of God. For best of all the scholar's privileges is that of "lending a hand." The scholar travels the road of life well equipped in all which can be helpful to others. He may not travel that road again (you remember the words of the old Quaker), and what he does for his neighbor must be done where his neighbor is. The noblest lives have left their traces, not only in literature or in history, but in the hearts of men. "If the teacher is to train others, still more must he train himself. The teacher's influence depends not on what he says, nor on what he does, but on what he is. He cannot be greater or nobler than himself. He cannot teach nobly if he is not himself noble." *

Not long ago, Professor William Lowe Bryan said: "Two summers since, in a Southern Indiana country neighborhood, I came upon the traces of a man. They were quite as distinct and satisfactory as a geologist

---

* Dr. Weldon, Head Master of Harrow.

could have wished for in the case of a vanished glacier. A good many years had passed away since the man was there, but the impression of his mind and character was still unmistakable. Long ago, when a boy of eighteen, with no special training and no extended education, this man went to Jefferson County to teach. What he did, what he said, what methods or text-books he used, what books or journals he read, I do not know. But if you will go there to-day, you will find in that community, among all classes and conditions of people, the most satisfactory evidence that that boy-teacher was a man, honest, sincere, energetic, inspiring.''

So have I found, as I have gone over this land of ours, traces here and there which show where a man has lived. In greater or less degree, as we come to know the inner history of some little town, we may find that from some past life its sons and daughters have drawn their inspiration; we may find that once within its borders there lived a man.

One word more: You will go to college, for better or for worse. Where shall you go? The answer to this is simple. Get the best you can. You have but one chance for a college education, and you cannot afford to waste that chance on a third-rate or fourth-rate school. There is but one thing that can make a college strong and useful, and that is a strong and earnest faculty. All other matters without this are of less than no importance.

Buildings, departments, museums, courses, libraries, catalogues, names, numbers, rules, and regulations do not make a university. It is the men who teach. Go where the masters are, in whatever department you wish to study.

Look over this matter carefully; for it is important. Go for your education to that school, in whatever State or country, under whatever name or control, that will serve your purposes best ; that will give you the best returns for the money you are able to spend. Do not stop with the middle-men. Go to the men who know ; the men who can lead you beyond the primary details to the thoughts and researches which are the work of the scholar.

Far more important than the question of what you shall study is the question of who shall be your teachers. The teacher should not be a self-registering phonograph to put black marks after the names of the lazy boys. He should be a source of inspiration, leading the student in his department to the farthest limit of what is already known, inciting him to make excursions in the greater realms of the unknown. A great teacher never fails to leave a great mark on every youth with whom he comes in contact.

Let the school do for you what it can ; and when you have entered upon the serious duties of life, let your own work and your own influence in the community be ever the strongest plea that can be urged in behalf of higher education.

II.

THE EVOLUTION OF THE COLLEGE CUR-
RICULUM.*

A RECENT writer on the German system of education, turning aside from his subject for a moment's
contemplation of the American system, says that the
most striking characteristic of the latter is, simply, its
want of system. Instead of being part of a definite
whole, well ordered or ill ordered, as the case may be,
each feature of the American system has been developed
with little regard to its relation to others.

Our colleges are English in birth and in tradition; our
universities caught their inspiration from Germany; while
our high schools and professional schools are native to
the soil — the former an outgrowth of the public-school
system, the latter of commercial enterprise. This confusion in development has been made more striking by our
misapplication of names, an example of which is seen
in our indiscriminate use of the terms "college" and
"university." In many a so-called "college" in America the chief work done is the teaching of the elements
of grammar and arithmetic. The "university idea"
is often regarded as fully met by the addition to such a
college of a normal school, a professor or two in law or
theology, and a self-supporting "college of music."

* President's Address, College Association of Indiana, 1887; reprinted from
"Science Sketches," (first edition; A. C. McClurg & Co., Chicago, 1888).

Yet, in spite of all eccentricities in name or form, we can recognize the existence of a certain definite type of school, which we may call the "American college." There are many variations in this type of school — variations due to geographical position, to the excess or deficiency in denominational zeal, or to the exigencies of the struggle for existence. For the fiercest conflicts of the average American college have not been with the black giant Ignorance, but with the traditional wolf at the door. In other words, this new country has not been liberal in its support of higher education; and, moreover, the funds available for this purpose have been used for planting, rather than for watering — to found a multitude of weak schools, rather than to make a few schools strong. There have been several reasons why this is so, and there are some few reasons why it has been well that it is so; but these questions I do not care to discuss now. The law of the survival of the fittest can be depended on to rectify sooner or later all mistakes of this kind. Suffice it to say, that we recognize the existence of the American. college, and that this college possesses a more or less definite college curriculum. Of the changes in this curriculum I wish now to speak.

I shall not try to follow out in detail its history prior to the time when its germs were brought to us from England in the landing of the Pilgrims. We can go back in England to the time when the philosophy of Aristotle constituted the college course. Then the entire curriculum was taught by a single teacher, the man of universal knowledge. This teacher, for the most part, gave his instruction by dictation. The students noted down the contents of old books, which the master himself had copied before; the place of the teacher was simply that of a medium of communication between the ancient manuscripts and their later duplicates.

With the revival of learning came the advent of the study of Latin as a language having a literature, and, later, the study of Greek, both Latin and Greek, as literary studies, being considered extremely dangerous as well as heretical at the time of their introduction into the curriculum. Both were then resisted by the full force of the conservative party of the day. After the revival of learning, came about with time the English college curriculum, with its tripos, or three pedestals, of Greek, Latin, and mathematics. Of this the American curriculum has been a lineal descendant.

The American college curriculum at the time when most of us became acquainted with it was a very definite thing, time-honored, and commanding a certain respect from its correspondence with the theory on which it was based. Its fundamental idea was discipline of the mind. Its mode of effecting this was, in large part, by shutting the student's eyes to the distracting and inconsequential present, and fixing his gaze on that which was great and good and hard to understand in the past. The main work of the course consisted of drill in grammar and mathematics, and the results of this training were bound together by a final exposition at the hands of the president of such of the speculations of philosophers as seemed to him safe and substantial. This work lasted — for reasons so old as to be long since forgotten — just four years, and it was preceded by a certain very definite amount of drill, of much the same kind, which was regarded as a necessary preliminary to the later work.

Whatever may be our opinion as to the desirability of such a course for ourselves, or for our sons or daughters, it is impossible not to regard the old-time classical course with a feeling of respect. It was based on a theory of education, and its promoters were loyal to this theory. If only the boys for whom its pigeon-holes were arranged could have been of uniform size and quality, the system would have been perfect. That it was not quite perfect was clearly the fault of human nature, which furnished a very variable article of boy for the educators to work upon, and caused them to reach by uniform processes widely different results. What these variations were is well known to us, and needs no explanation. We know that there are some boys whose natural food is the Greek root. There are others whose dreams expand in conic sections, and whose longings for the finite or the infinite always follow certain paraboloid or ellipsoid curves. There are some to whom the turgid sentences of Cicero are the poetry of utterance; and there are others who, with none of these tastes, grow and blossom in the sunlight of comradery, undisturbed by the harassing influences of books and bookish men. To all these kinds of students this old-time classical course brought satisfaction, and the days they spent in Princeton, or Harvard, or Amherst were the brightest of their lives. Such have rarely failed to try to provide for their children the same training which they found so satisfying to themselves.

But there were other students, not less fond of study, who were restless under these conditions. There were some to whom the structure of the oriole's nest was more marvelous, as well as more poetical, than the structure of an ode of Horace. There were others who found in modern history, or literature, or philosophy an inspiration which they did not draw from that which is old. By the side of this inspiration, the grammatical drill of the schools seemed a lifeless thing. And so it has happened that many whom we now regard as great in our literature or our science were held in low esteem in the colleges in which they graduated — if indeed they ever graduated at all. For the scale of marks connected with the college curriculum took little account of the soul of man, but only of the docility and regularity — virtues of themselves of no mean order — with which the college discipline was taken. And as these qualities are not alone the qualities which win success, either real or spurious, in after life, it came to be believed that college honors meant future failure — that the college valedictorian was the man who was never to be heard of again; and in this popular error, easily disproved by statistics, there was just enough of truth to keep it from being forgotten.

No doubt the ancient classical course was a powerful agency for culture to many — to most students, perhaps, who came within its influence. But it was not so to all. Culture is an elusive thing, and the machinery which will secure it for you may have no such effect on me. So, among the students of the old regime, some never found culture, and some found it only in a surreptitious study of the world outside. Complaints were not wanting that in this curriculum of Latin, Greek, mathematics, and a varnish of philosophy, not all the studies pursued were useful studies. Much of this complaint was unjust; for higher education is not learning a trade, nor is its purpose to enable its possessor to get a living. But some of this complaint has been just. No part of a man's education is of much value to him, unless it is in some way concerned with his future growth. Thousands of students never look at a Latin book after leaving college. This matters nothing, if the skill they have acquired in reading Latin gives them greater mastery over their future study or a deeper insight into the problems of life. This matters much, if this knowledge has in no wise given either insight or mastery. For in such case a knowledge of Horace and Homer would be as useless as the learning by heart of the laws of the Medes and the Persians or an enumeration in order of all the kings of Shanghai or Yvetot. The tree of knowledge is known by its fruits. "Culture," says Judge O. W. Holmes, "in the form of fruitless knowledge, I utterly abhor."

Now, to those who found culture, the college course had served its end; to others, it had not. It was good or bad, not in itself, but in its results. It is idle for us to say: " It is sufficient for all"; "It is sufficient for none." The discussion of these rival theses has not helped much in the solution of the educational problem.

Emerson says: " The ancient languages, with great beauty of structure, contain wonderful remains of genius, which draw, and always will draw, certain like-minded men, Greek men, and Roman men, in all countries, to their study ; but by a wonderful drowsiness of usage they had exacted the study of all men. Once (say two centuries ago) Latin and Greek had a strict relation to all the science and culture there was in Europe, and mathematics had a momentary importance at some era of physical science. These things became stereotyped as education, as the manner of men is. But the good spirit never cared for the colleges, and though all men and boys were now drilled in Latin, Greek, and mathematics, it had quite left these shells high and dry on the beach, and was now creating and feeding other matters at other ends of the world."

Thus, as the years went on, other sources of culture became more and more emphatic in their claims. The workers in the various fields of science, each year becoming more numerous and more active, opened out great vistas of the works of God, and he who had seen nothing of these might well have his claims to culture doubted. Philology, history, philosophy other than that stamped with the approval of the safe old masters, each put in its claims, as also the vast wealth of the literatures of modern Europe. A citizen of the republic must know something of the laws which govern national prosperity, and a teacher of the people should know something of the theory according to which people are taught. When these subjects are left out of the college curriculum, the clamor for their admittance becomes unbearably loud. If all are admitted, the same curriculum becomes like an American horse-car, with standing room only, and no space to turn around.

What shall the colleges do? Shut out these subjects they cannot; for to exclude all modern studies and modern ideas, to step out of the current of modern life, is practically to exclude all students. Rightly or wrongly, the students want these things, and sooner or later the American college must give what the students want. The supply must meet the demand, or there will be no demand. It is possible, although by no means sure, that we, as professors, know what is good for the student better than the student does himself; but unless we can convince him of that, we must let him have, to a great extent, his own way as to what his studies shall be. We can see that he does his work well, and we can help him in many ways; but the direction of his efforts must in the end rest with him.

The colleges of America stand in a different position in this regard from similar schools in England or Germany. These last are parts of a definite system. Their financial support is such that there is no need of paying any special attention to popular demands if these demands are deemed theoretically undesirable. Moreover, the college degree in England, and its equivalent in Germany, form a passport of admission to social, educational, or political privileges inaccessible to the man without this degree. Hence, entrance to the college, or gymnasium, or the university is, among the higher-educated classes in these countries, a matter of course to a much greater extent than can be the case in America. The Bachelor's degree in America, or even the Doctor's degree, carries no privileges of any sort worth the name. And in the long run it is well for America that it does not. Very few of our students would work for a degree if it were believed that the title were all they got. Thus it comes about that in America the average student goes to college or is sent to college for the help to be got from study, rather than for the sake of graduation. And he must be convinced, or his parents must be convinced, that this good is a real good, or he will not seek it. Thus the difference in the conditions under which our colleges work has tended to modify and modernize the curriculum more rapidly than has been the case in the corresponding schools in Europe.

Many devices have been adopted for dealing with the modern studies. Some have admitted them as extras, or, in the expressive language of a New York college president, as "side fixings," reserving the old-time tripos as the solid part of the scholastic meal. But no matter how little a hold these modern studies had, their presence has weakened the force of the old-time discipline. It is a law of physics that two bodies cannot occupy the same space, even though one of them be badly squeezed. And these subjects will submit to squeezing no better than the others. So part of the old course must be crowded out and part of the new must be admitted on terms of more or less perfect equality with the former, or else some degree of selection must be permitted, that students may choose between new and new or between new and old.

Another conceivable arrangement would be to omit none of the old work, but to lengthen the course, with each study added to the curriculum until each could receive a proper share of the student's attention. But this cannot well be done. Four years is the fixed length of the American college course; and this being an arbitrary thing, with no sort of reason for it, there can be no successful argument against it. Besides, we live in hurrying times; and to our students time is money, and the only money some of the best of them have. To the majority of those reached by our colleges, even the traditional four years seems a long time to spend in school after reaching manhood.

For a time, in various ways, it was sought to harmo-

nize the new education with the old. But the average
American college has finally adjusted itself to a second
phase in the history of the curriculum, which, for con-
venience, I may call "the patchwork" stage. In this
arrangement most of the higher mathematics has been
crowded out, the Greek has been shortened, and the
Latin also; while other subjects, in greater or less
amounts, have been more or less grudgingly admitted.
The amount and kind of these subjects are rarely determined by any prearranged plan or in accordance with
any sort of definite theory of education. As a matter of
fact, each college has a certain number of professors —
this determined by the board of trustees, in accordance
with real or imaginary needs of the college, or with the
real or imaginary claims of candidates for recognition.
Then, in the faculty meetings, each one of these professors claims what he wants, and receives what he can get,
in accordance with the law of the survival of the fittest
and the rule of the majority. Thus the curriculum in
each college becomes the resultant of many forces in a
condition of unstable equilibrium. It is altered, not in
accordance with the educational needs of the students, but
when one professor gives place in the faculty to another
more or less energetic or clamorous than he.

Occasionally in these patchwork courses of study, the
traces of some master-hand is visible — some method in
its madness, — which shows that somebody has tried to
work out an idea. But this is rarely so, I think; and in
the arrangement of most courses of study nothing higher
has been thought of than expediency and the exigencies
of compromise. From the struggle between the representatives of rival subjects in an overloaded course has

D

come about, by way of compromise, the establishment
of different courses of study, in each of which it is assumed that some scholastic faction will have the ascendency. In some colleges these various courses have been
put on an exact equality; but in most cases a more
or less positive pressure has been brought to bear in
favor of the classical course, and especially away from
the sciences. This is well, I think; for in most of our
colleges the instruction in science is still absurdly inade-
quate, and wholly valueless for the main end of scientific
instruction — the training of the judgment through its
exercise on first-hand knowledge. Wherever science
is yet in the meshes of bookishness it is best that students should be turned away from it. Wherever its
limbs are free it will hold its own, whatever the pressure
from those who do not value it as a factor in education.
In other words, a competent teacher of science need
never complain of obstacles in his way; for the odds are
all on his side. The same thing is true, I believe, of a
competent teacher in any other department. A growing
man incites growth; but even mold will not grow on a
fossil. Some fifteen years ago I heard a college president
boast that although his college had two other courses,
yet three-fourths of his students had been kept in the
classical course. My question was: "What sort of
teaching have you in science?" There was nothing
worth speaking of; only husks which the swine would
not eat, and the most hungry student could not.

As I have said, I do not think that the average college
curriculum, as we have known it in this second stage, is
the result of any sort of theory of education, of any
appreciation of the relative value of studies, or of any

thought as to the best order in which such subjects could be arranged. I have myself taken part in the preparation of too many such courses to have much respect for them. They are simply the results of an attempt to put a maximum of topics into a minimum of terms — to squeeze ten years of subjects into four years of time. The predominance of one group of subjects in a course reflects the predominance of some professor in that line of work. The idea of discipline, more or less prominent in the lower years, is usually forgotten entirely in the Junior and Senior years. The idea of the German schools, that the source of all power is concentration,— or, as Emerson expresses it, ''The one prudence in life is concentration; the one evil, dissipation,'' — was wholly abandoned. The theory arose that a college is not a place for thorough work of any sort. Its purpose is to give a broad and well-rounded culture; to train men to ''stand four-square to every wind that blows,''— such a culture as comes from a slight knowledge of many things, accompanied by thoroughness in nothing. Indeed, the desire of the student to know some one thing well was characterized as '' undue specialization,'' and every effort was made to induce the student to turn with equal eagerness from study to study — to physics, logic, Greek, or history,— equally interested, equally superficial, in each. The study of the text-book was exalted, and a subject was said to be completed when its alphabet and a few preliminary definitions were more or less perfectly memorized. Thus it came about that the average student regarded all studies with equal indifference. If a momentary spark of interest was evoked, it must fade out in a few days, as the subject in question gave place to some other. The procession moved in haste, and the student could not loiter if he kept his place in the line.

It was said in justification of this course of study, that the function of the college is to offer a taste of all sorts of knowledge. The student could try all, and select that which he liked best as the future work of his life. Thoroughness is for men, not boys, and it is a part of life-work rather than of school discipline. But every influence of the college was away from this end. The value of persistent study was never made known to the student. His professors were not specialists. They knew nothing from first-hand, and they undervalued in all ways the power which comes from knowing what one knows. So they taught only definitions, and classifications, and names, and dates, and scrap-work generally. There was little temptation to study; for the business of the professor was repetition, not investigation. It was in reference to such work as this that Agassiz said of Harvard College, some twenty years ago, that it was no university—"only a respectable high school, where they taught the dregs of learning." A candidate for a chair in an Illinois college demanded of the board of trustees that he must be allowed some time for study. He was not elected; for the board said that they wanted no man who had to study his lessons. They wanted a professor who knew already all that he had to teach. But a man contented with what he has learned from others can never be a great teacher. Only a man who has himself come into contact with nature at first-hand can lead others in the search for truth.

The true teacher, Dr. Coulter tells us, should be "an authority in the subject of his department, not a local

authority — any charlatan can be that, — but one among
his fellows. Such a man," he continues, "will have power
enough to be productive. The notion of a teacher as
one whose whole business is that of a pump, simply to
be pumped full from some reservoir, that he may fill the
little pitchers held up under his nose, may be true, but
it is dreadfully belittling. He should rather be a peren-
nial spring, where refreshing waters are constantly bub-
bling forth, a center and source of supply. The man
who has neither power nor inclination to work in his own
department, not only demonstrates his unfitness for teaching, but loses a great source of inspiration to his pupils.
Imagine the difference between two teachers before a
class; one carefully crammed with second-hand information which he is there to impart; the other in the flush
and fire of his own thought and work, stepping aside a
moment, as an artist, with palette and brushes in hand,
to explain the beauties of some great picture which he is
painting. The one is a taskmaster, the other an inspiration."

I am well aware that there is a cant of investigation,
as of religion and of all other good things. Germany,
for example, is full of young men who set forth to
investigate, not because they "are called to explore
truth," but because research is the popular fad, and
inroads into new fields the prerequisite to promotion.
And so they burrow into every corner in science, philology, philosophy, and history, and produce their petty
results in as automatic a fashion as if they were so many
excavating machines. Real investigators are born, not
made, and this uninspired digging into old roots and
"Urquellen" bears the same relation to the work of the

real investigators that the Latin verses of Rugby and Eton bear to Virgil and Horace. Nevertheless, it is true that no second-hand man was ever a great teacher. I very much doubt if any really great investigator was ever a poor teacher. How could he be so? The very presence of Asa Gray was an inspiration to students of botany for years after he had left the classroom. Such a man leaves the stamp of his greatness on every student who comes within the range of his influence.

One vice of the patchwork system is its constant implication that when, after a few weeks, a study is dropped, it is thereby completed,—as though any subject could be completed in a college course! For the first term or the first year spent in the study of any subject whatever, cannot give that subject. It gives only the elements of it, the dregs of it, the juiceless skeleton, on which future work must add the flesh and blood. Culture does not consist in the knowledge of any particular subject or set of subjects, nor is it the result of any order or method by which such studies are taken. Its essential feature is in the attitude which its possessor holds toward the world and toward the best that has been or can be thought or done in it. Its central quality is growth. The student gets nutriment from what he digests. "A cultivated woman," says a wise teacher of women, "can afford to be ignorant of a great many things, but she must never stop growing." Just so with the cultivated man. And to the young man or young woman who would grow, there is no agency so effective as the influence of a great teacher. "Under and around and above all mere acquirements," says the writer whom I have just quoted, "is this subtle infection of character, making the essence of the higher education as different from mere erudition as the fresh smell of the tender grape is from sheepskin." The school of all schools in America which has had the greatest influence on American scientific teaching was held in an old barn on an uninhabited island some eighteen miles from the shore. It lasted barely three months, and in effect it had but one teacher. The school at Penikese existed in the personal presence of Agassiz; and when he died, it vanished.

The final theory of the patchwork stage of the curriculum has been, as I have said, that of breadth of culture. The student should possess the elements of everything, that no part of the world should be a sealed book, that no part of his mind should be developed at the expense of any other. But the result was, in a general way, oftener confusion than culture. The bed-rock of the mind was never reached. So far as mental training was concerned, almost every result of this curriculum was distinctly inferior to that secured by the old classical course. In broadening and modernizing the curriculum, its sharpness as an implement was lost. The only real gain in the change, according to Professor Bain, has been "the relaxation of the grip of classicism." Another was, perhaps, that many who got nothing from the old course could, with the right kind of teachers, get something from this. But a criticism I once heard at one of our college exhibitions was still pertinent as to most of the work done by either professor or student under this regime: "What the boys want is to plow a little deeper. There is nothing like subsoiling."

From the second to the third stage in its history the curriculum of the American college is now passing.

This is marked by the advent of the elective system. It is impossible to study everything, or even many things, in four years. Thoroughness of any sort is incompatible with the so-called breadth of culture characteristic of the patchwork era. True breadth of culture comes from breadth of life, and four years in college cannot give it. The elective system, when carried out in its entirety, involves the following elements: (1) A substantial and thorough course of mental drill, preparatory to the college course,—this course being measured by its effect on the student's powers of study and of observation, not by the amount of grammar, algebra, and rhetoric which has been crammed into his head; (2) the placing of all subjects taught in the college course on an equality, so far as the degree is concerned.

The theory on which this system is based may be briefly stated as this: No two students require exactly the same line of work in order that their time in college may be spent to the best advantage. The college student is the best judge of his own needs, or, at any rate, he can arrange his work for himself better than it can be done beforehand by any committee or by any consensus of educational philosophers. The student may make mistakes in this, as he may elsewhere in much more important things in life; but here, as elsewhere, he must bear the responsibility of these mistakes. The development of this sense of responsibility is one of the most effective agencies the college has to promote the moral culture of the student. It is better for the student himself that he should sometimes make mistakes than that he should throughout his work be arbitrarily directed by others. Freedom is as essential to scholarship as to manhood. Not long since, I met a young German scholar, a graduate of a Prussian gymnasium, who has enrolled himself as a student of English in an American college. To him the free air of the American school was its one good thing. It develops a self-reliant manhood in the youth at an age at which the student of the gymnasium is yet in leading-strings. In furnishing the best of mental training in certain fixed and narrow lines, the German student is deprived of that strength which comes from self-help and individual responsibility. It is no mere accident that the need of severe college discipline to guard against the various forms of traditional college mischief has steadily declined with the advent of freedom of choice in study.

The elective system, too, enables the student to bring himself into contact with the best teachers,— a matter vastly more important than that he should select the best studies. And this system, therefore, involves a not unhealthy competition among the instructors themselves. Incompetent, superficial, or fossilized men will be crowded out or frozen out, and the law of the survival of the fittest will rule in the college faculties as elsewhere in nature.

The elective system has been adopted in greater or less degree by most of our leading colleges; while there are now very few schools, large or small, which do not make some provision for elective studies. That some degree of freedom of choice in higher education is desirable, no one now questions. The main differences of opinion relate to the proportion which these elective studies ought to bear to those which are absolutely required, and to the age or degree of advancement at which election is safe; for no one advocates freedom of choice from infancy. There is no such thing as a perfect curriculum, and all college courses must represent in some degree a compromise among varying influences, or else an adaptation to the needs of a certain class of students to the exclusion of others. All systems are liable to abuse; and as there have been many students who made a farce of the classical course, or who made it a mere excuse for four years spent in boating or billiards, or in social pleasures, so in the same way can a farce be made of the freedom allowed under the elective system.

Some of the chief deficiencies of the elective system may be summed up under the following heads:—

1. There are some students who, from pure laziness, select only the easiest studies, and go through college with the very easiest work which is possible. But this is no new thing, and it is not for such students that the colleges exist. The college should not obstruct the work of its earnest men to keep its idlers and sneaks from wasting their useless time. As Dr. Angell has said: "No plan will make the college career of lazy men brilliant. . . . The work of the college should be organized to meet the needs of the earnest and aspiring students, rather than the infirmities and defects of the indolent." That most students, as a matter of fact, do select the easiest studies is not true, as statistics certainly show. It is, in fact, simple nonsense to call any study easy, if pursued in a serious manner for a serious purpose. If any subject draws to itself the idlers solely because it is easy, the fault lies with the teacher. The success of the elective system, as of any system, demands the removal of inefficient teachers. The elective system can never wholly

succeed unless each teacher has the power and the will to enforce good work,— to remove from his classes all idle or inefficient students.

2. It is again objected that students having freedom of choice are likely to select erratic courses in accordance with temporary whims, rather than with any theory of educational development. This again is true; but it is likewise true that the course apparently the most erratic may be the one which brings the student in contact with the strongest men. If a Harvard student of a few years ago could have made his college course exclusively of botany, embryology, Greek, anatomy, and early English, it would seem a singular combination. It would sound differently if it were said that his teachers in college were chiefly Asa Gray, Goodwin, Holmes, Lowell, and Agassiz. It is also true, I think, that the average course as chosen by the students themselves is as capable of serious defense as the average established course evolved from the pulling, and hauling, and patching, and fitting of the average college faculty.

3. Another criticism is, that the elective system offers temptation to undue or premature specialization. This is true,— and premature specialization, like other forms of precocious virtue, is much to be deprecated. But experience does not lead me to think that the danger of "undue specialization" is at all a serious one. The current, in college and out, is all setting the other way. The fact that any man dares to specialize at all, shows that he has a certain independence of character; for the odds are against it. Specialization implies thoroughness, and I believe that thorough knowledge of something is the backbone of culture. Special knowledge of

any sort gives to each man the base-line by which other attainments may be measured; and this unit of measurement in scholarship can be acquired in no other way. There can be, I think, no scholarship worthy of the name without some form of special knowledge or special training as its central axis. The self-respect of the scholar comes from thorough work. The man who feels sure that he can know or that he can do something is assured at once from the danger of turgid conceit as from that of limp humility. He can hold up his head among men with a certainty as to his proper place among them.

I have often heard college graduates complain: "Oh, if I had only studied something in particular!" "Oh, if I had only learned how to study!" "Oh, if the time I have wasted in Latin had been spent in something else!" "Oh, if the time I have wasted in something else had been spent in Latin!" There are few college men of the present generation who would not be better scholars to-day if half their curriculum had been omitted (not much matter what half), and the time had been spent on the remaining subjects. But you may say: "Would you let a man graduate ignorant of chemistry, of Latin, of logic, of botany?" Well, yes, if superficiality in everything is the alternative. It is well for a scholar to know something of each of these and of each of the subjects in the most extended curriculum. But he purchases this knowledge too dearly if he buys it at the expense of thoroughness in some line of study in which a real interest has been awakened.

Then, again, with certain men in college the alternative is either a close specialization or no college life at all. Sometimes a man may wish in college to devote his entire time to a single subject — as physics or history, — making himself an authority on that subject, but without any effort for broad culture at all. This is not often a wise course; but, wise or not, no one will deny that a college career spent in this way is better than none at all, and in after years such men are rarely a source of shame to their Alma Mater. There is a certain well-known naturalist whom I could name, who some fifteen years ago was excluded from the university of his State — not because he was idle, or vicious, or weak, but because he wanted to spend most of his time in the study of natural history. The college had then no place for such a man as that. It had no use for bird-knowledge, though it came out strong on irregular verbs. But the same college is proud of him now, and twelve years later granted the degree it had refused. Who is to say that it was better for him to leave college than that he should be allowed to follow his own bent? No knowledge comes amiss to an investigator; but no investigator can afford to sacrifice his speciality for the sake of breadth of culture. Thoroughness is the main point, after all, and should take precedence over versatility. I do not mean to be understood as advocating narrowness of sympathy or narrowness of culture of any sort. The broadest education is none too broad for him who aspires to lead in any part of the world of thought. But the forces of the mind, to continue the figure, should not be scattered in guerrilla bands, but marshaled toward leadership.

An advantage of the elective system, which has been too often overlooked, is its reflex influence on the teacher. If a good teacher is the essential element in a good school, then anything which helps to make his work better, more thorough, or more inspiring, is of the greatest value to the student. The great teachers of the world, for the most part, have not been, and could not be, drill-masters. The man who works with realities cannot become a martinet. In the elective system, the teacher deals with students who have chosen his courses for the love of the work or for love of him. Contact with these classes is a constant stimulus and a constant inspiration. No teacher can ever do his best on required work or prescribed courses, and the best that is in his teacher it is the student's right to receive.

There is still much to be said in favor of the college in which discipline pure and simple is made the chief aim of all the work. In such a school those subjects — languages, sciences, and philosophy — which serve the ends of training best should be taught, and such subjects only. Whether anything more suitable for this purpose than the ancient classics and mathematics has yet been found, I shall not try to say; but the aims of such a course should be the same in kind as that of the classical curriculum. It may perhaps be possible to teach better things and in a better way than was done in the classical schools; but all attempts at combining in a prescribed curriculum mental discipline and a wide range of subjects must result in failure, so far as training the mind is concerned; you cannot teach everything to every student — either the student or the college must choose.

4. Still another criticism of the elective system is just the reverse of this. The elective system permits undue scattering. It allows the student to flit from one subject to another, thus acquiring versatility without real training. This seems to me a more serious fault than any of

the others. It can be remedied in part by a system of major and minor studies, or a division of the work into specialities which must be pursued for a considerable length of time, and electives which may be dropped after a simple mastery of their elements. Some such arrangement as this seems to me a desirable check upon the elective plan, as it tends to insure persistence in something, while retaining most of the flexibility of the latter system.

Some of the weakest features of our college system center, it seems to me, about the conventional term of four years, and the conventional Bachelor's degree. Students are encouraged to work for the degree, rather than for culture; all work of the student is estimated by the bulk, rather than by the quality. In an ideal condition of things, the student's work ought not to be estimated at all. Marks and terms are clumsy devices, more suitable for measuring cordwood than culture. The degree is the official seal of completion set on something which in the nature of things can never be completed. For the college is not a machine for filling the student with wisdom and learning. It is, at best, a place for self-culture. All culture is self-culture, or it is no culture at all. Libraries, apparatus, museums, teachers even, are useless to the student, unless the student use them. Teachers give inspiration and criticism; fellow-students do the same: but the road to wisdom is a solitary road, to be traversed in Indian file.

We may lay on the Bachelor's degree at once too much stress or too little : too much, for the degree is treated as if it were an end in itself; too little, for every college in our land gives this degree to men whose sole claim to higher education consists in a four years' residence in a college town — a four years' "exposure to scholastic influences." They make their count of marks on the college books, and if, by hook or crook, they can keep "regular," the march of time will carry them through. Then, again, the competition for numbers among our would-be "populous schools" often leads to discrepancies between the actual requirements and those laid down in the published catalogues. Thus low standards are adopted for mere numbers' sake. And besides the reputable institutions, all sorts of mushroom establishments, in private hands, have in the Middle West been authorized by law to grant the Bachelor's degree with practically no scholastic requirements at all.

When the colleges in the patchwork era attempted to teach in four years a little of everything, it was found that by the same process a little of everything could likewise be given in two years, or even in one year, by carrying the process of condensation a little farther. I received a letter not long ago from the president of an alleged college in Kansas — a school which gives the Bachelor's degree on a course a year or two long, begun at any time, and with no special preparation. He said that he had exactly one year of daily recitations to devote to all the sciences, each completed in turn. He was especially anxious to make no mistake in the logical order of arrangement of these sciences — whether it should be chemistry, physics, geology, physiology, zoology, and botany, or whether the order would be better if reversed. Of course, the only answer I could make was, that the order was of little importance, and that if a year was all the time he had for all of them, it would be better to omit any five, or at least any four, and to spend his time on the rest. But to drop any science would be to drop the pretense of offering a liberal education. I have no doubt that he found room at last to work all of them in, and a term of astronomy and one of political economy besides!

I quote from the catalogue of an alleged "college" in Indiana a statement in regard to its "scientific course" of one year's duration, which leads to a degree called "Bachelor of Science": "The graduates [of this course] are polished speakers as well as accurate mathematicians, thorough scientists, and accomplished Latin scholars. Graduates from this department fill good positions, and are everywhere known as leaders, because of their energy, perseverance, enthusiasm, and never-ceasing activity,"—and so on. The so-called "insurmountable barrier" to a degree "formed by the long courses of the colleges and State normal schools" is at once blown away, and all obstacles which debar indolence and ignorance from the privileges of scholarship once for all removed.

I have a friend in the city of Indianapolis, a most estimable gentleman, in the real-estate and rental business, who some forty years ago received from the Legislature of the State of Indiana a charter which constituted him a "university," entitled to hold two hundred thousand dollars in property free from all taxes, "to confer all academic degrees, and to enjoy all the rights and privileges of the most favored institution." This gentleman has been merciful to his fellow-citizens. He has gone about his business, and has conferred no degrees, not even on himself. But he has the legal right to do it; and this incident shows with what laxness the laws of our States view the granting of collegiate degrees. Such is the degradation

E

of the Bachelor's degree, which has already brought the name of American graduate into contempt!

Still, at the best, the Bachelor's degree is an empty name. It is not in America, as in Europe, a key to any sort of personal advancement. And it is better that it should be so. It is better for each man to stand on his own merits as shown by his own life, not as attested by any college faculty. "The student may flourish his college diploma," says Dr. J. P. Lesley, "but the world cares little for that baby badge." In certain educational circles, perhaps, a college degree is a help, or, rather, it may represent a certain minimum of culture which is expected of all its members. We suppose that a college professor must hold a college degree. But this is not always the case. I can count on my fingers, taking every one, a list of some of the ablest of American college teachers to-day, who have never been graduated from any college. Most of these hold honorary degrees, it is true; but such degrees are empty tributes of the college to success of one sort or another, won without the college's help.

It is true, no doubt, that the hope of a degree coaxes some men to stay in college longer than they otherwise would. This seems a good thing — but is it? Higher education is not working for a degree. It may be incompatible with it. It is putting a cheap price on culture to induce the student to take it, not because he wants it, but because he wants something else. If a student's work is purely perfunctory, the sooner he leaves it for something real the better. If the degree is merely a bait to lure him on, it is unworthy alike of the college and of the student.

Shall we, then, abandon the Bachelor's degree, and give to each student merely the certificates of the professors under whom he has studied? Some day, perhaps, but certainly not yet. The French writer, Joubert, has said: "All truth it is not well to tell; but all truths it will be well to tell when we can all tell them together." There is wisdom in this saying. Degrees are childish things, and it would be well to lay them aside; but this we cannot do till we can all do it together. Some ten years ago, Chancellor Gregory, of the State University of Illinois, held the opinion that the college degrees were undesirable adjuncts of college training. It was decided that by the University of Illinois no degrees should be granted. But this decision worked adversely to the interests of the college. Many students came there to study, who went elsewhere to complete their work. The degree might be useless, but the students wanted it. Their lack of a degree was a hindrance in securing positions; and they went to other colleges where degrees were still given. The times were not ready for this change, and the giving of degrees has been resumed — wisely, I think, — by the institution in question.

The same end is being reached in another way by the University of Virginia and some other colleges of the South. In these schools the Bachelor's degree receives little or no attention, being practically merged in the higher requirements for the degree of Master of Arts. By merging both these in the still higher degree of Doctor of Philosophy, we have a condition similar to that in the German universities, where only the Doctor's degree is now given. Toward this condition our universities are tending; and, through the change of the college into the university, the Bachelor degree may in time disappear. But this reform — if reform it be — can be the work of no one man or one school. It must come as a natural result of the development of the college.

So much for the phases, past and present, of the college curriculum in America. What of the future? Will there be a fourth, a fifth, a sixth stage in its development; or is the system now full grown, and the elective plan, as we know it, its full fruition?

We can be sure that the world is still moving. Nothing is stable, nothing is perpetual, nothing is sufficient. With the new needs and the new men of the future will come new departments, new methods, and new ideas. The curriculum, in its original sense of a little race-course, with thirty-six hurdles to be leaped in thirty-six months, with a crown of laurel berries at the end, will very soon be no more. Special courses of study in as many special departments are already taking its place. The traditional four years of college training will disappear, and with it the sharp lines which have so long set apart the Freshmen, Sophomores, Juniors, and Seniors. Later on, but not far in the next century, the Bachelor's degree will cease to be regarded; its kindred, the Master's degree, is dying already, and the degree of Doctor, the worthiest of all, has no elements of immortality. All these things are forms, and forms only, not substance; and the substance of our higher education is fast outgrowing them. College marks, college honors, college courses, college degrees, all these things belong, with the college cap and gown and the wreath of laurel berries, to the babyhood of culture. They are part of our inheritance from the past, — from the time when scholarship was not manhood, when the life of the student had no relation to the life of the world.

The American college of the future will be a place for self-culture. The chief need of a college organization is to bring great teachers together, that their combined influence may effect results which cannot be reached in isolation. In other words, the use of a college is to produce a college atmosphere,— such an atmosphere as forms itself around all great teachers everywhere. The various so-called colleges and universities in America will gradually differentiate into universities and preparatory schools, and the line of direction will ultimately depend on the available resources rather than on the ambition of the school. To do university work requires better-trained professors, and many more of them, than to teach the elements of Latin, Greek, and mathematics. This means more salaries and larger salaries than are now paid. Schools ill endowed or not endowed at all cannot attempt this. Those who can do it will do it. The ideas of "*Lehrfreiheit*" and "*Lernfreiheit*,"— freedom of teaching and freedom of study,— on which the German university is based, will become a central feature of the American college system.

The college as a separate factor in our educational system must in time disappear, by its mergence into the preparatory school, on the one hand, and into the university, on the other. In our Western States, the high school and the State university already complete the educational series. The college, as such, is already out of the current of the educational stream. The most striking feature of recent educational history has been the growth of the State universities, the consummate flower of the public-

school system. It needs no prophet to see that the ultimate growth of each and every one of these into real
universities, worthy of our country and worthy of the
coming twentieth century, is inevitable.

With time, we shall reach in America a condition of
things not unlike that seen in Germany, where nothing
intervenes between the public high school or gymnasium,
in which all work is prescribed, and the university itself,
in which all work is free. The position of the preparatory school in this connection is by no means one to be
despised. A strong high school is far more valuable to
the community than a weak college. The work of the
secondary schools is the foundation of everything higher.
It should be broadened and deepened so as to include all
subjects which experience shows to belong to the acces-
sory groundwork of higher education. I need not go
over a list of these subjects. The future will make its
own list, and the efforts of the colleges will not change
it. But we may be sure that the ultimate demand of the
colleges will be for students who are trained to see and
to think, not for students who can merely remember.
The best studies for college preparation should be the
best studies for those who do not go to college. They
are studies which give power and skill, not those which
merely give information.

But here, it seems to me, is one of the chief difficulties
in the way of our colleges, East and West. No school,
it seems, is content to be a preparatory school; no school
is content to train for future work elsewhere. Each one
aims to give a general education; to be a university in a
small way, a "university for the poor,"—a poor university. In the words of Lowell: "The public schools

teach too little or too much : too little, if education is to go no farther; too many things, if what is taught is to be taught thoroughly. And the more they seem to teach, the less likely is education to go farther; for it is one of the weaknesses of democracy to be satisfied with the second best if it appear to answer the purpose tolerably well, and to be cheaper, as it never is in the long run.'' In other words, the high schools, too, are in the patch-work era, and popular feeling tends to keep them there, to satisfy by a show of education the vast majority of their students who are likely to go no farther. The growth in educational systems is from above downwards, and the right kind of preparatory schools will arise only in response to the demands of real universities. In his-torical sequence, Oxford must precede Rugby, and the German university must come before the gymnasium. The American high school will not reach, I think, the standard of the German gymnasium, which gives train-ing not inferior in amount or kind to that of our best classical colleges; for in the American system the univer-sity methods of work will begin lower down than in Ger-many. This is associated with our qualities as a people, as compared with those of the Germans. The American youth of twenty-one is more independent, more self-reliant, and, so far as his relation to the world is con-cerned, more mature than the average German student is at twenty-five. America is, of all lands, the land of prot-estantism; and in education, as in other things, every American is a law unto himself. This fact has its bad side as well as its good side, but is a fact nevertheless; and as educators of Americans, we must take it into account.

The old forms in education are passing away; the old barriers are being taken down; the old restraints are being removed or relegated to the days of boyhood and girlhood. All this we can see, for it takes place before our eyes; it is taking place under our hands, and this whether we wish it or not. The college boy is becoming a man, and the college woman now stands beside him. Not all are ready for freedom, perhaps, who have freedom thrust upon them. There are not a few students to whom an enforced discipline is the only road to scholarship. But, with all imaginable drawbacks, our college work in America yields each year better results than it has ever yielded before. We may be sure that in the future, even more than in the past, the American college, the American university, will stand in the front rank of civilizing influences.

III.

THE NATION'S NEED OF MEN.*

IF the experiment of government by the people is to be successful, it is you and such as you who must make it so. The future of the republic must lie in the hands of the men and women of culture and intelligence, of self-control and of self-resource, capable of taking care of themselves and of helping others. If it falls not into such hands, the republic will have no future. Wisdom and strength must go to the making of a nation. There is no virtue in democracy as such, nothing in American-ism as such, that will save us, if we are a nation of weak-lings and fools, with an aristocracy of knaves as our masters.

There are some who think that this is the condition of America to-day. There are some who think that this republic, which has weathered so nobly the storms of war and of peace, will go down on the shoals of hard times; that we, as a nation, cannot live through the nervous exhaustion induced by the financial sprees of our-selves and others. We are told that our civilization and our government are fit only for the days of cotton and corn prosperity. We are told that our whole industrial system, and the civilization of which it forms a part, must be torn up by the roots and cast away. We are told that

---

* Address to the class of 1894, Leland Stanford Junior University; pub-lished in the Popular Science Monthly, December, 1894.

the days of self-control and self-sufficiency are over, and
that the people of this nation are really typified by the law-
less bands rushing blindly hither and thither, clamoring
for laws by which those men may be made rich whom all
previous laws of God and man have ordained to be poor.

In these times it is well for us to remember that we
come of hardy stock. The Anglo-Saxon race, with its
strength and virtues, was born of hard times. It is not
easily kept down; the victims of oppression must be of
some other stock. We who live in America, and who
constitute the heart of this republic, are the sons and
daughters of "him that overcometh." Ours is a lineage
untainted by luxury, uncoddled by charity, uncorroded
by vice, uncrushed by oppression. If it were not so, we
could not be here to-day.

When this nation was born, the days of the government of royalty and aristocracy were fast drawing to a
close. Hereditary idleness had steadily done its work,
and the scepter was already falling from nerveless hands.
God said: "I am tired of kings; I suffer them no more."
And when the kings had slipped from their tottering
thrones, as there was no one else to rule, the scepter fell
into the hands of the common man. It fell into our
hands, ours of this passing generation, and from us it
will pass on into yours. You are here to make ready for
your coronation, to learn those maxims of government,
those laws of human nature, without which all adminis-
trations must fail; ignorance of which is always punish-
able by death. If you are to hold this scepter, you must
be wiser and stronger than the kings; else you, too, shall
lose the scepter as they have lost it, and your dynasty
shall pass away.

For more than a century now the common man has
ruled America.   How has he used his power?   What
does history tell us of what the common man has done?
It is too soon to answer these questions.   A hundred
years is a time too short for the test of such gigantic
experiments.   Here in America we have made history
already—some of it glorious, some of it ignoble; much
of it made up of the old stories told over again.   We have
learned some things that we did not expect to learn.   We
find that the social problems of Europe are not kept away
from us by the quarantine of democracy.   We find that
the dead which the dead past cannot bury are thrown up
on our shores.   We find that weakness, misery, and
crime are still with us, and that wherever weakness is
there is tyranny also.   The essence of tyranny, we have
found, lies not in the strength of the strong, but in the
weakness of the weak.   We find that in the free air of
America there are still millions who are not free—
millions who can never be free under any government or
under any laws, so long as they remain what they are.

The remedy for oppression, then, is to bring in better
men, men who cannot be oppressed.   This is the remedy
our fathers sought; we shall find no other.   The problem
of life is not to make life easier, but to make men stronger,
so that no problem shall be beyond their solution.   It
will be a sad day for the republic when life is easy for
ignorance, indolence, and apathy.   It is growing easier
than it was; it is too easy already.   There is no growth
without its struggle.   Nature asks of man that he use his
manhood.   If a man puts no part of his brain and soul
into his daily work—if he feels no pride in the part he
is taking in life,—the sooner he leaves the world the

better.   His work is the work of a slave, and his life the
waste of so much good oxygen.   The misery he endures
is nature's testimony to his worthlessness.   We cannot
save him from nature's penalties.   Our duty toward him
may be to temper justice with mercy.   This is not the
matter of importance.   Our duty toward his children is
to see that they do not follow his path.   The grown-up
men and women of to-day are, in a sense, past saving.
The best work of the republic is to save the children.
The one great duty of a free nation is education —
education, wise, thorough, universal; the education, not
of cramming, but of training; the education which no
republic has ever given, and without which all republics
must be in whole or in part failures.   If this generation
should leave as its legacy to the next the real education,
training in individual power and skill, breadth of outlook on the world and on life, the problems of the next
century would take care of themselves.   There can be no
collective industrial problem where each man is capable
of solving his own individual problem for himself.

In this direction lies, I believe, the key to all industrial
and social problems.   Reforms in education are the greatest of all reforms.   The ideal education must meet two
demands: it must be personal, fitting a man or woman
for success in life; it must be broad, giving a man or
woman such an outlook on the world as that this success
may be worthy.   It should give to each man or woman
that reserve strength without which no life can be successful, because no life can be free.   With this reserve the
man can face difficulties, because the victor in any
struggle is he who has the most staying power.   With
this reserve, he is on the side of law and order, because

only he who has nothing to lose can favor disorder or misrule. He should have a reserve of property. Thrift is a virtue. No people can long be free who are not thrifty. It is true that thrift sometimes passes beyond virtue, degenerating into the vice of greed. Because there are men who are greedy — drunk with the intoxication of wealth and power, — we sometimes are told that wealth and power are criminal. There are some that hold that thrift is folly and personal ownership a crime. In the new Utopia all is to be for all, and no one can claim a monopoly, not even of himself. There may be worlds in which this shall be true. It is not true in the world into which you have been born. Nor can it be. In the world we know, the free man should have a reserve of power, and this power is represented by money. If thrift ever ceases to be a virtue, it will be at a time long in the future. Before that time comes, our Anglo-Saxon race will have passed away and our civilization will be forgotten. The dream of perfect slavery must find its realization in some other world than ours, or with a race of men cast in some other mold.

A man should have a reserve of skill. If he can do well something which needs doing, his place in the world will always be ready for him. He must have intelligence. If he knows enough to be good company for himself and others, he is a long way on the road toward happiness and usefulness. To meet this need our schools have been steadily broadening. The business of education is no longer to train gentlemen and clergymen, as it was in England; to fit men for the professions called learned, as it has been in America. It is to give wisdom and fitness to the common man. The great reforms in edu-

cation have all lain in the removal of barriers. They
have opened new lines of growth to the common man.
This form of university extension is just beginning. The
next century will see its continuance. It will see a change
in educational ideals greater even than those of the revival of learning. Higher education will cease to be the
badge of a caste, and no line of usefulness in life will be
beyond its helping influence.

The man must have a reserve of character and purpose. He must have a reserve of reputation. Let others
think well of us; it will help us to think well of ourselves.
No man is free who has not his own good opinion. A
man will wear a clean conscience as he would a clean shirt,
if he knows his neighbors expect it of him. He must have
a reserve of love, and this is won by the service of others.
"He that brings sunshine into the lives of others cannot
keep it from himself." He must form the ties of family
and friendship; that, having something at stake in the
goodness of the world, he will do something toward making the world really good.

When an American citizen has reserves like these, he
has no need to beg for special favors. All he asks of
legislation is that it keep out of his way. He demands
no form of special guardianship or protection. He can
pay as he goes. The man who cannot has no right to
go. Of all forms of greed, the greed for free lunches,—
the desire to get something for nothing,— is the most de-
moralizing, and in the long run most dangerous. *The
flag of freedom can never float over a nation of deadheads.*

Then, again, education must take the form of real
patriotism — of public interest and of civic virtue. If a
republic be not wisely managed, it will fail as any other

corporation would; it will only succeed as it deserves success.

The problems of government are questions of right and wrong; they can be settled only in one way. They must be settled right. Whatever is settled wrong comes up for settlement again, and this when we least expect it. It comes up under harder conditions, and compound interest is charged on every wrong decision. The slavery question, you remember, was settled over and over again by each generation of compromisers. When they led John Brown to the scaffold, his last words were: "You would better — all you people of the South — prepare yourselves for a settlement of this question, that must come up for a settlement again sooner than you are prepared for it. You may dispose of me now very easily," he said; "I am nearly disposed of now; but this question is still to be settled — this negro question, I mean; the end of that is not yet."

This, John Brown said, and they settled the problem for the time by hanging him. But the question rose again. It was never settled until at last it was "blown hellward from the cannon's mouth." Then it was found that for every drop of negro blood drawn by the lash, a thousand drops of Saxon blood had been drawn by the sword.

Thus it is with every national question, large or small. Thus it will be with the tariff, with finance, with the civil service. Each question must be settled right, and we must pay for its settlement. It is said that fifteen per cent of the laws on the statute books of the States of the Union stand there in defiance of acknowledged laws of social and economic science. Every such statute is blood

poison in the body politic.   Around every such law will
gather a festering sore.   Every attempt to heal this sore
will be resisted by the full force of the time-servers.   Such
statutes are steadily increasing in number — concessions
by short-sighted legislatures to the arrogant monopolist,
the ignorant demagogue, or the reckless agitator.   This
must stop.   ''They enslave their children's children who
make compromise with sin,'' or with ignorance, or with
recklessness.   ''The gods,'' said Marcus Aurelius, ''are
at the head of the administration, and will have nothing
but the best.''

> "My will fulfilled shall be;
> In daylight or in dark,
> My thunderbolt has eyes to see
> Its way home to the mark!"

It was the dream of the founders of this republic that
each year the people should choose from their number
''their wisest men to make the public laws.''   This was
actually done in the early days; for our first leaders were
natural leaders.   The men who founded America were
her educated men.   None other could have done it.   But
this condition could not always last.   As the country
grew, ignorance came and greed developed; ignorance
and greed must be represented, else ours would not be
a representative government.   So to our congresses our
people sent, not the wisest, but the men who thought as
the people did.   We have come to choose, in our law-
makers, not rulers, but representatives; we ask not wisdom, but watchfulness for our personal interests.   So we
send those whose interests are ours; those who act as our
attorneys.   And just as the people do this, so do the
great corporations, who form a large part of the people

and control a vastly larger part. And as the corporations command the best service, they often send as their attorneys abler men than the people can secure. And so it has come about that demagogues and special agents make up the body of lawmakers in this country, and this in both parties alike. They represent, not our wisdom, but our business. They are the reflex of the people they represent; no better, and certainly no worse. Those whose interest lies in the direction of good government alone are too often unrepresented.

In this degree republican government has failed. For this failure there is again but one remedy — education. If the people are to rule us, the people must be wise. We must have in every community men trained in social and political science. We must have men with the courage of their convictions; only education can give real convictions. We must have men who know there is a right to every question as well as many wrongs. We must have men who know what this right is; or, if not knowing, who know how the right may be found. Very few men ever do that which they know and really believe to be wrong. Most wrongdoing comes from a belief that there is no right, or that right and wrong are only relative.

Professor Powers has said: "We are no longer guided by wise men. We are guided by wise men's wisdom after we have reviewed it and decided that it is wisdom. An increasing proportion of our people are fairly independent in their thought, and vigorous in their assertion of their convictions. These men — common human men — without their knowledge or consent, come into the world charged with the awful responsibility of managing inter-

F

ests compared with which the tasks of the old gods of Olympus were but as children's play.''

If representative government is ever to bring forward wisdom and patriotism, it will be because wisdom and patriotism exist and demand representation. In this direction lies one of the most important duties of the American university. Every question of public policy is a question of right and wrong. To such questions all matters of party ascendency, all matters of individual advancement must yield precedence. There is no virtue in the voice of majorities. The danger of ignorance or indifference is only intensified when rolled up in majorities. Truth is strong, and error is weak, and the majorities of error melt away under the influence of a few men whose right acting is based on right thinking. Right thinking has been your privilege; right acting is now your duty; and at no time in the history of the world has duty been more imperative than now.

IV.

THE CARE AND CULTURE OF MEN.*

"THE best political economy," Emerson tells us, "is the care and culture of men." Culture is not coddling, but training,—not help from without, but growth from within. The harsh experience of centuries has shown that men are not made by easy processes. Character is a hardy plant. It thrives best where the north wind tempers the sunshine.

The life of civilized man is no simple art,— no automatic process. To make life easy is to destroy its effectiveness. The civilization to which we are born makes heavy demands upon those who take part in it. Its rights are all duties; its privileges are all responsibilities. Its risks are terrible to those who do not make their responsibilities good. And these responsibilities are not individual alone. They fall upon all who are bound together in social or industrial alliance. If we are to bear one another's burdens, we must see that we lay upon ourselves no unnecessary burdens by our indifference or our ignorance. There is no safety for the republic, no safety for the individual man, for whom the republic exists, so long as he or his fellows are untrained or not trained aright.

So there is no virtue in educational systems unless these systems meet the needs of the individual. It is

* Address to the class of 1895, Leland Stanford Junior University.

not the ideal man or the average man who is to be trained; it is the particular man as the forces of heredity have made him.   His own qualities determine his needs. "A child is better unborn than untaught."   A child, however educated, is still untaught if by his teaching we have not emphasized his individual character, if we have not strengthened his will and its guide and guardian, the mind.

The essence of manhood lies in the growth of the power of choice.   In the varied relations of life the power to choose means the duty of choosing right.   To choose the right, one must have the wit to know it and the will to demand it.   In the long run, in small things as in large, wrong choice leads to death.   It is not "punished by death," for nature knows nothing of rewards and punishments.   Death is simply its inevitable result.   No republic can live—no man can live in a republic in which wrong is the repeated choice either of the people or of the state.

All education must be individual — fitted to individual needs.   That which is not so is unworthy of the name. A misfit education is no education at all.   Every man that lives has a right to some form of higher education. For there is no man that would not be made better and stronger by continuous training.   I do not mean, of course, that the conventional college education of to-day could be taken by every man to his advantage.   Still less could the average man use the conventional college education of any past era.   Higher education has seemed to be the need of the few because it has been so narrow. It was born in the days of feudal caste.   It was made for the few.   Its type was fixed and pre-arranged, and those whose minds it did not fit were looked upon by the colleges as educational outcasts. The rewards of investigation, the pleasures of high thinking, the charms of harmony were not for the multitude. To the multitude they must be accessible in the future; but not as gifts — nothing worth having was ever a gift, — rather as rights to be taken by those who can hold them.

To furnish the higher education that humanity needs, the college must be broad as humanity. No spark of talent man may possess should be outside its fostering care. To fit man into schemes of education has been the mistake of the past. To fit education to man is the work of the future.

The traditions of higher education in America had their origin in social conditions very different from ours. In the Golden Age of Greece, each free man stood on the back of nine slaves. The freedom of the ten was the birthright of the one. To train the tenth man was the function of the early university. Only free men can be trained. A part of this training of the tenth in the early days was necessarily in the arts by which the nine were kept in subjection.

The universities of Paris, and Oxford, and Cambridge were founded to educate the lord and the priest. And to these schools and their successors, as time went on, fell the duty of training the gentleman and the clergyman. Only in our day has it been recognized that the common man had part or lot in higher education. For now he has come into his own, and he demands that he, too, may be noble and gentle. His own lord and king is the common man already, and in the next century we shall see him installed as his own priest. And through higher education he must gain fitness for his work, if he gain it at all. And he must gain it; for the future of civilization is in his hands. The world cannot afford to let him fail. All the ages have looked forward to the common man as their "heir apparent." The whole past of humanity is staked on his success.

The old traditions are not sufficient for him. The narrow processes by which gentlemen were trained in medieval Oxford are not adequate to the varied demands of the man of the twentieth century. He is more than a gentleman. Heir to all the ages he must be; and there are ages since, as there were ages before, the tasks set in these schools became stereotyped as culture. The need of choice has become a thousand-fold greater with the extension of human knowledge and human power. The need of choosing right is steadily growing more and more imperative. If the common man is to be his own lord and his own priest in these strenuous days, his strength must be as great, his consecration as intense as it was with those who were his rulers in ruder and less trying times. The osmosis of classes is still going on. By its silent force it has "pulled down the mighty from their seats, and has exalted them of low degree." Again educate our rulers. We find that they need it. They have, in the aggregate, not yet the brains, nor the conscience, nor the force of will that fits them for the task the fates have thrown upon them.

If the civilization of the one is shared by the ten, it must increase tenfold in amount. If it does not, the Golden Age it seems to represent must pass away. To hold the civilization we enjoy to-day is the work of higher education. Every moment we feel it slipping from our hands. Hence, every moment we must strive for a fresh hold. "Eternal vigilance," it was said of old, "is the price of liberty." And this was what was meant. The perpetuation of free institutions rests with free men. The masses, the mobs of men, are never free. Hence the need of the hour is to break up the masses. They should be masses no longer, but individual men and women. The work of higher education is to put an end to the rule of the multitude. To tyranny confusion is succeeding, and the remedy for confusion is in the growth of men who cannot be confused.

The university of to-day must recognize the need of the individual student as the reason for its existence. If we are to make men and women out of boys and girls, it will be as individuals, not as classes. The best field of corn is that in which the individual stalks are most strong and most fruitful. Class legislation has always proved pernicious and ineffective, whether in a university or in a state. The strongest nation is that in which the individual man is most helpful and most independent. The best school is that which exists for the individual student. A university is not an aggregation of colleges, departments, or classes. It is built up of young men and women. The student is its unit. The basal idea of higher education is that each student should devote his time and strength to what is best for him; that no force of tradition, no rule of restraint, no bait of a degree should swerve any one from his own best educational path. As Melville Best Anderson has said, "The way to educate a man is to set him at work; the way to get him to work is to interest him; the way to interest him is to vitalize his task by relating it to some form of reality."

No man was ever well trained whose own soul was not wrought into the process. No student was ever brought to any worthy work except by his own consent.

So the university must not drive, but lead. Nor, in the long run, should it even lead; for the training of the will is effected by the exercise of self-guidance. The problem of human development is to bring men into the right path by their own realization that it is good to walk therein. The student must feel with every day's work that it has some place in the formation of his character. His character he must form for himself; but higher edution gives him the materials. His character gathers consecration as the work goes on, if he can see for himself the place of each element in his training. Its value he has tested, and he knows that it is good, and its results he learns to treasure accordingly.

Individualism in education is no discovery of our times. It was by no means invented at Palo Alto; neither was it born in Harvard nor in Michigan. The need of it is written in the heart of man. It has found recognition wherever the "care and culture" of man has been taken seriously.

A Japanese writer, Uchimura, says this of education in old Japan: " We were not taught in classes then. The grouping of soul-bearing human beings into classes, as sheep upon Australian farms, was not known in our old schools. Our teachers believed, I think instinctively, that man *(persona)* is unclassifiable; that he must be dealt with personally — *i. e.* face to face, and soul to soul. So they schooled us one by one — each according to his idiosyncrasies, physical, mental, and spiritual. *They knew each one of us by his name.* And as asses were never harnessed

with horses, there was but little danger of the latter being beaten down into stupidity, or the former driven into
valedictorians' graves. In this respect, therefore, our
old-time teachers in Japan agreed with Socrates and
Plato in their theory of education. So naturally the relation between teachers and students was the closest one
possible. We never called our teachers by that unap-
proachable name, Professor. We called them *Sensei,*
men born before, so named because of their prior birth,
not only in respect of the time of their appearance in
this world, which was not always the case, but also of
their coming to the understanding of the truth. It was
this, our idea of relationship between teacher and student,
which made some of us to comprehend at once the inti-
mate relation between the Master and the disciples which
we found in the Christian Bible. When we found written
therein that the disciple is not above his master, nor the
servant above his lord; or that the good shepherd giveth
his life for his sheep, and other similar sayings, we took
them almost instinctively as things known to us long
before.''

Thus it was in old Japan. Thus should it be in new
America. In such manner do the oldest ideas forever
renew their youth, when these ideas are based not on
tradition or convention, but in the nature of man.

The best care and culture of man is not that which
restrains his weakness, but that which gives play to his
strength. We should work for the positive side of life.
We should build up ideals of effort. To get rid of vice
and folly is to let strength grow in their place.

The great danger in democracy is the seeming predominance of the weak. The strong and the true seem

to be never in the majority. The politician who knows the signs of the times understands the ways of majorities. He knows fully the weakness of the common man. Injustice, violence, fraud, and corruption are all expressions of this weakness. These do not spring from competition, but from futile efforts to stifle competition. Competition means fair play. Unfair play is the confession of weakness.

The strength of the common man our leaders do not know. Ignorant, venal, and vacillating the common man is at his worst; but he is also earnest, intelligent, and determined. To know him at his best, is the essence of statesmanship. His power for good may be used as well as his power for evil. It was this trust of the common man that made the statesmanship of Abraham Lincoln. And under such a leader the common man ceased to be common. To know strength is the secret of power. To work with the best in human nature is to have the fates on your side.

"A flaw in thought an inch long," says a Chinese poet, "leaves a trace of a thousand miles." If collective action is to be safe, the best thought of the best men must control it. It is the ideal of statesmanship to bring these best thoughts into unison. The flaw in the thought of each one will be corrected by the clear vision of others. And this order and freedom, clear vision and clean acting, we have the right to expect from you. Knowledge is power, because thought is convertible into action. Ignorance is weakness, because without clearness of purpose action can never be effective.

The best political economy is the care and culture of men. The best-spent money of the present is that which is used for the future. The force which is used on the present is spent or wasted. That which is used on the the future is repaid with compound interest. It is for you to show that effort for the future, of which you are the subjects, is not wasted effort. That you will do so we have no shadow of doubt. If its influence on you and you only were the whole of the life of the university we love, it would be worth all it has cost. The money and the effort, the faith and devotion these halls have seen would not be wasted. The university will live in you. You are her children — first-born, and it may be best-beloved, — and in the ever-widening circle of your work she shall rejoice. For your influence will be positive, and therefore effective. It stands for the love of man and the love of truth. No one can love man aright who does not love truth better. And in the end these loves are alike in essence.

The foundation of a university, as Professor Howard has told us, may be an event greater in the history of the world than the foundation of a state. By its life is it justified. The state at the best exists for the men and women that compose it. Its needs can never be the noblest, its aims never the highest, because it can never rise above the present. Its limit of action is that which now is. The university stands for the future. It deals with the possibilities of men, with the strength and virtue of men which is not yet realized. Its foundation is the co-operation of the strong, its function to convert weakness into strength. The universities of Europe have shaped the civilization of the world. The universities of the world will shape the growth of man so long as civilization shall abide.

V.

THE SCHOLAR IN THE COMMUNITY.*

A LL civilized countries live under a government by popular opinion. In proportion as public opinion is wise and enlightened, the government will be enlightened and wise. In other words, the people will always have as good a government as their intelligence and patriotism deserve, and no better. In the long run government can be made better only by the improvement of the public opinion on which it rests. This can be done only by the spread of knowledge and the development of the moral sense. It is one of the chief duties of the University to send out men who, by their personal influence, shall help in the making of good citizens. The management of a great republic in these days is not a simple thing. Our nation has within itself a host of evil forces, and these forces will destroy it if their influence is not met by still more potent forces working together for good. We must know these evil influences, their origin, their power, and their results, if we are to do effective work against them. In this need lies the reason for your education.

The nation and the university have the right to expect of you, as educated men and women, to stand everywhere as forces on the side of good government. Not that you should be good citizens merely; that you should

* Address to the Class of 1893, Leland Stanford Jr. University.

observe the laws, deal justly with your neighbors, pay your debts, support your families, and keep out of jail. All this we expect of men in general; but as you have had opportunities not granted to the majority, the State has the right to expect more of you. It asks not only that you should break none of its laws, but that you should help to make and sustain wise laws; that you should stand for good, for right living, right thinking, and right acting in the community. It expects you to do this, even at a sacrifice of your own personal interests. If you should not so stand, your education has been a losing bargain. It has simply "sharpened your claws and whetted your tusks" that you may the more easily prey upon your unenlightened neighbors.

What then shall the State expect of you more than of the others? Where shall you stand when the count is taken in politics, in morals, in religion? If you are to help raise the standard of public opinion, you must address yourself to the work in earnest. You must not stand aloof from the people it is your duty to help. Yet, standing with the masses, you should never lose yourself in the mass. You must keep your own compass and know your own road. The mass will move to the left when your instincts and principles tell you to go to the right. You may find it a hard struggle, and may seem to fail at last; but a force once exerted can never be lost.

It is not your duty to join yourself to organizations which can take away any part of your freedom. It is not your duty to vote the ticket of my party, nor of your party, nor that of any one of the time-honored political organizations into which men naturally fall. For you and I know that the questions which divide the great parties of a free country are not, as a rule, questions of morals or good citizenship. The sheep are never all on one side, nor the goats on the other. Party divisions are based, for the most part, on hereditary tendencies, on present expediencies, and hopes of temporary gain, and too often on the distribution of power and plunder, of power to plunder. When your party is led by bad men, or when its course is headed in the wrong direction, your State expects you as educated men to know it.

Your State expects you to have the courage of your convictions. Your State expects you to have the power to stand alone — to bolt, if need be, when other modes of protest fail. You will not win friends by asserting your manhood against partisan pressure. You will not pave the way to a vote of thanks or a nomination to Congress, but you will keep your own self-respect, and some day, when the party recovers its senses, you will see it come in full run in your direction.

One duty of the scholar in politics is to serve as an antidote to the thick-and-thin partisan — the rock-ribbed Bourbon of any party, who learns nothing, and scruples at nothing. A good citizen, as has been well said, cannot vote an unscratched ticket. The man who does so, in whatever party, leaves in the course of years few sorts of rascals, public or private, unsupported by his vote. The men whom your vote helps to elect are properly regarded as your representatives, and the knave, the trickster, the gambler, the drunkard, the briber, the boss, should not rightfully represent you. If such do represent you, it would be better for our country if you were left unrepresented, and the State has made a losing bargain in educating you.

I do not plead for political isolation. That you stand aloof from the majority, is no proof that you are right and they are wrong. For the most part, we believe, the feeling of the majority is not far from right. The great heart of the republic beats true. To doubt this would be to despair of popular government. But whether right or wrong, the majority of the party are not the keepers of your conscience. Your conscience is your own. "I went into this convention," said a brave man once, "a free man, with my own head under my own hat, and a free man I meant to come out of it." The opinions of the majority are molded by the few. That among these few who would mold opinion you should stand, is a reason for your training in the science of government. In all questions of public or private policy, be yourself, no matter who your grandfather was, no matter who your neighbor may be. If you are born and bred in any party, think of these things. A hereditary yoke is ignoble; shake it off, and then, when once a free man, you may resume your place, if you choose. If there must be a hereditary partisanship in your family, be you the man to start it. Be the first in your dynasty, and encourage your son to be the first in his.

But your State expects more of you than mere independence of hereditary prejudices. Let it never be said of you: "It is for his interest to do so and so; therefore we can count on him. He lives in the First Ward; therefore he believes in prohibition. He lives in the Sixth Ward; therefore his vote is for free whisky. He will make by this thing; therefore he favors that course of action."

It is much easier to be independent of political bosses than
to be free from the dictation of your own selfish instincts.
But the good citizen is superior to the prejudices of his
locality, to the selfish interests of his trade.   The good
man is a citizen of the State, not of the Sixth Ward—not of
the iron county, nor of the raisin county, nor of the State
merely, nor of the United States.   The good citizen is a
citizen of the world; itself, as citizenship improves, becoming one vast community, the greatest of all republics.
For true patriotism is not a matter of waving flags and
Fourth of July orations.   It lies not in denouncing England nor in fighting Chile; not in cock-crowing nor in
bull-baiting.   It consists in first knowing what is true
about one's own community or country, and then in the
willingness to sink one's personal interest in the welfare
of the whole.   All patriotism which involves neither
knowledge nor self-devotion is a worthless counterfeit.

We have the right to expect the scholar to serve as an
antidote to the demagogue.   You have been trained to
recognize the fetiches and bugaboos of the past; you
should know those of the present.   Notions as wild, if
not as wicked, as the witchcraft that haunted Salem two
hundred years ago still vex our American life.   The
study of history is your defense against these.   As "the
running stream, they dare na' cross," kept off the witches
of old, so will your studies in this field defend you from
bugaboos, alive or dead.   You hold the magic wand before which the demagogue is silent and harmless.   It is
your duty and privilege to use it for the people's good.

It is true that America is not the best governed of the
civilized nations.   You know that this is so.   You know
that America's foreign policy is weak, vacillating, ineffi-

cient. You know that her internal policy is lavish, careless, unjust. You know that we no longer send, as in the old days, "our wisest men to make the public laws." You know that our legislative bodies, from the board of aldermen to the United States Senate, are not always bodies of which we are proud. You know that their members often are not men in whom the people have confidence. Our civil service has been one of the worst "on the planet"; our foreign service has been the laughingstock of Europe. Our courts of justice, on the whole the soundest part of our Government, are not all that they should be. Too often they are neither swift nor sure. Too often the blindfold goddess who rules over them is quick to discern the pressure of the finger of gold on the "wrong side of the balances." Our currency fluctuates for the benefit of the gambler, who thrives at the laborer's cost. In all this our own California offers no exception. The history of her government is a short one, but it is long with the records of misrule and corruption. Her average of general intelligence is high. Her average of special knowledge is low, and equally low is her standard of patriotism.

All these things we know, and worse, and they vex us and discourage us, and some there are among us who wish that we had a heaven-descended aristocracy, an aristocracy of brains at least, who could take these things out of the people's hands, out of your hands and mine, and make them and keep them right. I do not feel thus. It is better that the people should suffer, with the remedy in their own hands, than that they should be protected by some power not of themselves. Badly though the people may manage their own affairs, the

G

growth of the race depends upon their doing it. We would rather the people would rule ill through choice than that they should be ruled well through force. The Reign of Terror gives more hope for the future than the reign of the good King Henry. The story of the decline and fall of empires is the story of the growth of man.

It is not that the laws of England should be made better that Gladstone took into partnership, as law-makers, two millions of England's farmers and workmen who can barely read or write. The laws for a time, at least, will not be as good, but those for whom the laws are made will be better, and the good of the people is the object of law. It is not our confidence in Irish wisdom and prudence that leads every American to approve of Home Rule in Ireland. It is our sympathy with Irish manhood and our belief that Irish manhood can manage its own affairs. It is not that our Southern States should be better governed that three millions of freedmen, little more intelligent in the mass than the dog or horse with which a few years before they had been bought and sold, were given the right to vote. No better for the State, perhaps; for an ignorant vote is a cowardly vote, and a vote which money will buy. No better for the State, but better for humanity, that her laws should recognize the image of God hidden in each dusky skin. For lawlessness, turbulence, misgovernment is better than prosperity with its heel on the neck of a silent race which cannot rise nor speak.

But all government by the people is made better when the people come to know and feel its deficiencies. No abuse can survive long when the people have located it. When the masses know what hurts them, that particular wrong must cease. Its life depends upon its appearing in the disguise of a public blessing. Straight thinking, as you have learned, comes before straight acting, and both we expect of you. To you, as educated men and women, the people have a right to look. They have a right to expect your influence in the direction of the ideal government, the republic in which government by the people shall be good government as well; the government from which no man nor woman shall be excluded, and in which no man nor woman shall be ignorant, or venal, or corrupt.

The influence of the university life is in the direction of high ideals. The trained mind is the best keeper of the clear conscience. It is the duty of the university to fill the student's mind with high notions of how his personal, social, and political life ought to be conducted and to lead him toward discontent with that which is on a lower plane. You have all heard it said that certain reforms in American life are advocated only by college professors and by boys just out of college. It is said that these notions of college boys would be admirable in Utopia, but are ridiculous in nineteenth-century America. We are told that self-seeking and corruption are essential elements in our American life. That in our political and social battles we must not be squeamish, but must fight our adversaries as devils are said to fight each other — with fire. Of course, this charge of Utopianism is in the main true, and I trust that it may remain so. The Utopian element is one which our life sorely needs. We have fought the devil with fire long enough. Too long have we attempted good results by evil means. Too long has the right been grandly victorious through bribery, falsehood, and fraud, till we are more afraid of the bad means of our friends than the bad ends of our adversaries.

What though all reform seem Utopian,—does that absolve you?   Unless your soul dwells in Utopia, life is not worth the keeping.   Your windows should look toward heaven, not into the gutter.   You should stand above the level of the world's baseness and filth.   If our scholars do not so stand — if our training end in the production merely of sharper manipulators than those we had before (and we know there is an undercurrent in our college life tending just in that direction), then the sooner we bar our windows and don our striped uniforms, the better for the country.

But we need not take this dark view of the future.   We know that, on the whole, training makes for virtue. There is a natural connection between "Sweetness and Light."   We know that whatever leads the youth to look beyond the narrow circle in which he stands, is his best safeguard against temptation.   We know that if the youth fall not, the man will stand.   I shall not argue this question.   I assume it as a fact of experience, and it is this fact which gives our public-school system, of which my life and yours is in some degree a product, the right to exist.   "A dollar in a university," says Emerson, "is worth more than a dollar in a jail.   If you take out of this town the ten honestest merchants, and put in ten rogues, with the same amount of capital, the rates of insurance will soon indicate it, the soundness of the banks will show it, the highways will be less secure, the schools will feel it, the children will bring home their little dose of poison, the judge will sit less firmly on his bench, and his decisions will be less upright; he has lost so much support and constraint, which we all need, and the pulpit will betray it in a laxer rule of life." If taking from the community ten good men and replacing them with bad men work this evil, what will come from doing the reverse? If we add ten good men — one good man — to any community, the banks, the courts, the churches, the schools will feel it as an impulse toward better things.

The statesmanship of every nation has regarded the development of higher education as a plain duty to itself. The great universities of the world have arisen, not from the overflow of riches, but from the nation's need of men. The University of Leyden was founded in the darkest days of Holland's history as the strongest barrier Holland could raise against Spanish oppression — as the most effective weapon she could place in the hands of William the Silent.

For the State — that is, every man in the State — is helped and strengthened by all that makes its members wiser, better, or more enlightened. That you are educated, if educated aright, tends to raise the price of every foot of land around you. When Emerson, and Hawthorne, and Thoreau lived in Concord, this fact was felt in the price of every city lot in Concord. Men from other towns were willing to pay money in order to live near them. When a smart lawyer, a few years ago, was elected governor of Massachusetts, there were men who left that State rather than that he should be their governor. You and I are not so sensitive, perhaps; but however that may be, the election of a bad man as governor will be felt in the falling price of land and houses, in the falling price of honesty and truth in the markets of the nation.

As in political, so in social life, should the student stand as a barrier against materialism. Not alone against the elaborate materialism of the erudite philosopher. Its virus, dry and dusty, attenuated by its transfer from Germany, can rarely do much harm. But there is a subtler materialism which pervades our whole life. It sits in the cushioned pews of our churches, as well as in our marts of trade. It preaches the gospel of creature comforts and the starvation of the spirit. It preaches the gospel of selfhood, instead of the law of love. It asks of all the scholar should hold dear,— of truth, and beauty, and goodness, and sweetness, and light,— what are these things worth? If they will bring no money in this world, nor save our souls in the next, we want nothing of them. Wherever you go after you leave the college halls, you will feel the chill of this materialism. You must keep your sympathies warm, and your soul open to all good influences, to keep it away.

There is, too, a sort of skepticism about us against which the scholar should be proof. Once the skeptic was the man simply who had his eyes open; the man who questioned nature and life, and from such question-ing has all of our knowledge come. But questioning with eyes open is not the same as doubting with eyes closed. There is a doubting which saps the foundation of all growth, which cuts the nerve of all progress. It is the question of Pilate, who doubted—"What is truth?" Whether, indeed, any truth exists? And whether, after all, being is other than seeming?

Every robust human life is a life of faith. Not faith

in what other men have said and thought about life, or death, or fate; but faith that there is something in the universe that transcends man and all man's conceptions of right and wrong, and which it is well for man to know.

Some forty years ago a president of the University of Indiana is reported to have said: "The people insist on being humbugged; so it is our duty to humbug them." Great is the power of Humbug, and many and mighty are his prophets! Do you never believe this. A pin-prick in the ribs will kill the charlatan, but the man who is genuine throughout is clad in triple armor. To him and to his teachings will the people turn long after the power of humbug is forgotten. The studies you have followed as a scholar should teach you to know and value truth. You have found some things which you should know as true, judged by any tests the world can offer.

In his relations with others, the scholar must be tolerant. Culture comes from contact with many minds. To the uncultured mind, things unfamilar seem uncouth, outlandish, abhorrent. A wider acquaintance with the affairs of our neighbor gives us more respect for his ideas and ways. He may be wrong-headed and perverse; but there is surely something we can learn from him. So with other nations and races. Each can teach us something. In civilized lands the foreigner is no longer an outcast, an object of fear or abhorrence. The degree of tolerance which is shown by any people toward those whose opinions differ from their own is one of the best tests of civilization. It is a recognition of individuality and the rights of the individual in themselves and in others.

I need not dwell on this. The growth of tolerance is one of the most important phases in the history of mod-

ern civilization.   The right of freedom of the mind, the
right of private interpretation, is a birthright of humanity.
As the scholar has taken a noble part in the struggle
which has won for us this freedom, so should he guard
it in the future as one of his highest possessions.   It is
each man's right to hew his own pathway toward the
truth.   If there be in this country a town, North, South,
East, West, on the banks of the Yazoo, or the Hudson,
or the Sacramento, where an honest man cannot speak
his honest mind without risk of violence or of social
ostracism, in that town our freedom is but slavery still,
and our civilization but a barbarism thinly disguised.

The man who speaks may be a sage or a fool; he may
be wise as a serpent, or harmless as a calf; he may please
us or not: yet, whatever he be, his freedom of speech is
his American's birthright.   To words, if you like, you
can answer with words.   The whole atmosphere is yours,
from which to frame your replies.   If you are right, and
he is wrong, so much the stronger will your answer be.
But the club, the brick, the shotgun, or the dynamite
bomb are not the answer of the free man or the brave.
They convince nobody; and of all oppressive laws, the
law which is taken in the hands of the mob is the most
despotic and most dangerous.

The scholar should never allow himself to become a
mere iconoclast.   He has no strength to waste in con-
troversy.   Truth is non-resistant because its enemies
cannot last.   There is not much to be gained from
tearing down.   Build something better, and the old will
disappear of itself.

When a righteous man attempts to reform society by
attacking an unrighteous man, the public forms a ring

around the two, to see that there is fair play, and that truth and falsehood are given alike a fair show. Soon the public ceases to be interested in the question of who is right, and becomes interested in who is the best fellow.

The people have the right to expect of the scholar growth. One of the saddest products of the college is that which in science is called "arrested development." When the student is transplanted from the hotbed of the college to the cold soil of the world, his growth some-times ceases, to the disappointment of his friends and the dismay of those who have faith in higher education. Without that perseverance which thrives under adver-sity, your attainments in college will avail you little.

You have reached one port in the journey of life; and of this achievement you have the right to be proud. But the first port is not the end of the voyage. The great ocean is still beyond you, and the value of the voyage in the long run is proportionate to the distance of the port for which you are bound. It takes a longer preparation and a larger equipment for a voyage to the Cape of Good Hope than for a sail to the "Isle of Dogs."

The value of a life is measured by its aim rather than by its achievement. Loftiness of aim is essential to lofti-ness of spirit. Nothing that is really high can be reached in a short time nor by any easy route. Most men, as men go, aim at low things, and they reach the objects of their ambitions. They have only to move in straight lines to an end clearly visible. Not so with you. You are bound on a quest beyond the limit of your vision. There are mountains to climb, rivers to ford, deserts to cross on your search for the Holy Grail. The end is never in sight. You have always to trust and struggle on, parting company at every step with those who have chosen more accessible goals or are diverted from the great quest by chance attractions. "Heaven is not reached by a single bound," nor by him who knows not whither he is going.

That your aims in life are high, that you are pledged to a life of effort and growth, is shown by your presence here. Were it not so, you would never have pressed thus far onward. You would be with the hundreds and thousands of your contemporaries who are satisfied with inferior aims reached in an inferior way.

We all recognize this fact, even though we may not have put the thought into words. The banks recognize it. Without a dollar in your pocket, you can borrow money on the strength of your purpose. Many of you have already done this. You may have to do it again. It is right that you should. Strength of purpose is a legitimate capital. By your own desires and aspirations you are enriched. In a free country there can be but one poor man — the man without a purpose.

What you have done thus far is little in itself. You have reached but the threshold of learning. Your education is barely begun, and there is no one but you who can finish it. Your thoughts are but as the thoughts of children, your writings but trash from the world's waste-paper basket. Nothing that you know, or think, or do but has been better known or thought or done by others. The work of your lives is barely begun. You must continue to grow as you are now growing before you can serve the world in any important way. But the promise of the future is with you. You have the power and will of growth. The sunshine and rain of the next century will fall upon you. You will be stimulated by its breezes, you will be inspired by its spirit.

It is not an easy thing to grow. Decay and decline is easier than growth—so the trees will tell you. Growth is slow, and hard, and wearisome. The lobster suffers the pangs of death every time he outgrows and sheds his shell; but each succeeding coat of armor is thicker, and stronger, and more roomy. So with you. You will find it easier not to develop. It will be pleasanter to adjust yourself to old circumstances and to let the moss grow on your back. The struggle for existence is hard; the struggle for improvement is harder; and some there are among you who sooner or later will cease struggling. Such will be the cases of arrested development—those who promised much and did little, those whose education did not bring effectiveness. Be never satisfied with what you have accomplished, the deeds you can do, the thoughts you can think. Such satisfaction is the sting of old age, the feeling that the best is behind us, and that the noble quest is over forever.

The scholar shall be a man of honor, one whom men may trust. Once a king wrote to his queen, after a disastrous battle: "Madam, all is lost—all but our honor." When honor is saved a battle can never be lost. But in many of the battles and sham fights of the world—in most of those, perhaps, in which you will be called to take part,—the honor on one side or the other is the first thing to be lost. Some men, in entering public life, lay aside their consciences as Cortez burned his ships, that they may not be tempted to retreat toward honor and decency. People say, as you have heard, that the sense of honor in our republic is waning; that

sentiment in politics or business is a thing of the past.
Certainly, from Franklin, and Hamilton, and Knox, and
Jay to some public servants we have seen, the fall has
been great, and the descent to Avernus seems easy. We
hear sometimes of men who possess the old-fashioned
ideas of honor, and we associate these men with the
knee-breeches, and wigs, and ruffles of the same old-
fashioned times. The moral law is growing flexible with
use, and parts of it, like the Blue Laws of Connecticut,
are already out of date. See to it that it is not so with
you. In any contest fair play is better than victory. The
essence of success is fair play.

As honest men and women, you will often find yourselves in opposition to those who regard themselves as
leaders of reform.*   A cause founded on sentiment, even
though it be righteous sentiment, cannot succeed all at
once, and never, unless controlled by wisdom. Political
expediency may be a wiser guide than feeling alone.
There is some truth in the paradox that sentimentality in
politics is more dangerous than venality, and that the
venal man is our safeguard against the idealist and enthu-
siast. Venality, with all its evils, is conservative, hence

* Professor H. H. Powers has said : "A knowledge of the magnitude and
complexity of the causes of social phenomena tends to disparage panaceas
and all hasty efforts for social improvement. However much we may believe
in the control of social evolution by reason and human effort, a study of
society cannot but convince us that changes must be slow to be either whole-
some or permanent, and that effort spent on merely proximate causes is
ineffectual. These conclusions are not agreeable to those who organize cru-
sades. It is one of the painful incidents of science that the student is so
often called upon to part company with the reformer. The fervid appeals and
enthusiastic championship by which he seeks to enlist men into a grand
reforming mob grate harshly on the ears of one who sees the difficulties of
bettering society, while the other sees only its desirability. After a few vain
attempts to inoculate a little science into these reformers while they are
charging at double-quick, the student is apt to give up the attempt and to
seem henceforth unfriendly to reform."

opposed to ill-considered action. "*Laissez-faire*" is now a discredited principle. It is no longer possible to let things take their course when so many men try to find out what is right, and use every effort to bring it about. But we must remember that men can do only what is possible. All unscientific or sentimental tinkering with society, and law, and government is still "*laissez-faire.*" The blind effort to do the impossible effects nothing. It is only the whirl of the water in the eddy of the stream, which in no way hastens or changes its flow. Man must first learn the direction of the currents. The efforts he puts forth must be in harmony with these currents, else his labors may hinder, and not help, real progress. The opposite of *laissez-faire* is not action simply, but action based on knowledge.

To be known as an apostle or as the devotee of some special idea, often prevents a man from learning or from growing. The apostle fears to confuse his mind with the results of the study of social forces. The scholar cannot ignore these forces, and must be prepared to reckon with each one. But this does not justify indifference or obstruction. Wisdom and sobriety arise from the efforts of wise and sober men. Wise and sober you should be, if you are rightly educated.

Not all of you will leave your names as a legacy to your country's history. The alumni roll of your Alma Mater may be at last the only list that remembers you; but if you have been a center of right living and right thinking, if the character of your neighbors is the better for your having lived, your life mission will have been fulfilled. No man or woman can do more than that. "True piety," as you have heard to-day, "consists in reverence for the gods and help to men.* Therefore help men. Seek that spiritual utilitarianism whose creed is social perfection, and foster that intelligent patriotism which chastens because it loves.''

* Professor George Elliott Howard.

VI.

THE SCHOOL AND THE STATE.*

THE very essence of republicanism is popular education. There is no virtue in the acts of ignorant
majorities, unless by dint of repeated action the majority is no longer ignorant. The very work of ruling
is in itself education. As Americans, we believe in government by the people. This is not that the people are
the best of rulers, but because a growth in wisdom is sure
to go with an increase in responsibility.

The voice of the people is not the voice of God; but
if this voice be smothered, it becomes the voice of the
demon. The red flag of the anarchist is woven where
the people think in silence. In popular government, it
has been said, ignorance has the same right to be represented as wisdom. This may be true, but the perpetuity
of such government demands that this fact of representation should help to transform ignorance into wisdom.
Majorities are generally wrong, but only through the experience of their mistakes is the way opened to the permanent establishment of right. The justification of the
experiment of universal suffrage is the formation of a
training-school in civics, which, in the long run, will bring
about good government.

Our fathers built for the future — a future even yet
unrealized. America is not, has never been, the best

* Address given on Charter Day of the University of California, at Berkeley,
March, 1893.

governed of civilized nations. The iron-handed dictator-
ship of Germany is, in its way, a better government than
our people have ever given us. That is, it follows a more
definite and consistent policy. Its affairs of state are conducted with greater economy, greater intelligence, and
higher dignity than ours. It is above the influence of
the two arch-enemies of the American State — the cor-
ruptionist and the spoilsman. If this were all, we might
welcome a Bismarck as our ruler, in place of our succession of weak-armed and short-lived Presidents.

But this is not all. It is not true in a changing world
that that government "which is best administered is
best." This is the maxim of tyranny. Good government
may be a matter of secondary importance even. Our
government by the people is for the people's growth.
It is the great training-school in governmental methods,
and in the progress which it insures lies the certain pledge
of better government in the future. This pledge, I
believe, enables us to look with confidence on the gravest
of political problems, problems which other nations have
never solved, and which can be faced by no statesmanship other than

> "The right divine of man,
> The million trained to be free."

And, in spite of all reaction and discouragement, every
true American feels that this trust in the future is no idle
boast.

But popular education has higher aims than those involved in intelligent citizenship. No country can be
truly well governed in which any person is prevented,
either by interference or by neglect, from making the
most of himself. "Of all state treasures," says Andrew

D. White, "the genius and talent of citizens is the most precious. It is a duty of society to itself, a duty which it cannot throw off, to see that the stock of talent and genius in each generation may have a chance for development, that it may be added to the world's stock and aid in the world's work."

This truth was recognized to its fullest degree by the founders of our Government, and so from the very first provision was made for popular education. The wisdom of this provision being recognized, our inquiry is this: How far should the State go in this regard? Should popular education cease with the primary schools, or is it the duty of the State to maintain all parts of the educational system — primary schools, secondary schools, colleges, technical and professional schools, and the schools of instruction through investigation, to which belong the name of university?

There have been from time immemorial two schools in political economy — two opposite tendencies in the administration of government; the one to magnify, the other to reduce the power and responsibility of the State. The one would regard the State as simply the board of police. Its chief function is the administration of justice. In other matters it would stay its hands, leaving each man or institution to work out its own destiny in the struggle for existence. The weaker yield, the stronger move on. Progress must come from the inevitable survival of the fittest. "*Laissez-faire*," (let it alone) is the motto, in all times and conditions.

The opposite tendency is to make the State not just, but benevolent. In its extreme the State would become a sort of generous uncle to every man within it. It would

H

feed the hungry, clothe the needy, furnish work for the idle, bounties for those engaged in losing business, and protection for those who feel too keenly the competition inherent in the struggle for existence. It would make of the State a gigantic trust, in which all citizens might take part, and by which all should be lifted from the reach of poverty by official tugging at the common boot-strap.

Somewhere between these two extremes, I believe, lies the line of a just policy. Aristotle says that "it is the duty of the state to accomplish every worthy end which it can reach better than private enterprise can do." Accepting this view of the State's duty, let us see to what extent education comes within its function. Education is surely a worthy object. Mill says: "In the matter of education, the intervention of government is justifiable, because the case is not one in which the interest and judgment of the consumer are a sufficient security for the goodness of the commodity."

In other words, unless the State take the matter in hand and make provision for something better, a cheap or poor article of education may be furnished, to the injury of the people. This authority of the State over the lower schools has been jealously guarded by the American people, and the result of this care has been one of the chief objects of our national pride. On the other hand, the higher schools, and to a still greater degree the professional schools, of America, have been allowed to shift for themselves, in accordance with the doctrine of "*laissez-faire.*" What has been the result?

"The common school is the hope of our country." So we all agree, and this sentence stands on the letter-heads of half of the school officers in the West. It is the common-school education that elevates our masses above the dignity of a mob. Such slight knowledge at least is essential to the coherence of the State.

"An illiterate mass of men, large or small," says President White, "is a mob. If such a mob had a hundred millions of heads — if it extends from ice to coral, it is none the less a mob : and the voice of a mob has been in all time evil; for it has ever been the voice of a tyrant, conscious of power, unconscious of responsibility."

"The great republics of antiquity and of the medieval period failed," he continues, "for want of that enlightenment which could enable their citizens to appreciate free institutions and maintain them. Most of the great efforts for republican institutions in modern times have been drowned in unreason, fanaticism, anarchy, and blood. No sense of responsibility can be brought to bear on a mob. It passes at one bound from extreme credulity toward demagogues to extreme skepticism towards statesmen; from mawkish sympathy towards criminals to bloodthirsty ferocity against the innocent, from the wildest rashness to the most abject fear. To rely on a constitution to control such a mob would be like relying on a cathedral organ to still the fury of a tornado. Build your constitution as lordly as you may, let its ground-tone of justice be the most profound, let its utterances of human right be trumpet-tongued, let its combination of checks and balances be the most subtle, yet what statesman shall so play upon its mighty keys as to still the howling tempest of party spirit, or sectional prejudice, or race hatreds, sweeping through an illiterate mob crowding a continent?"

The reformer Zwingli saw three hundred years ago

that Protestantism meant popular education, and popular education meant republicanism. It meant popular education because the recognition of the right of the individual to form his own opinions made it the duty of the state to give him the means of making these opinions intelligent. It meant republicanism, because the right of private interpretation in religion gave the people the right to opinions of their own in matters of politics. Where the people have a mind, they must, sooner or later, have a voice.

Long ago, at the end of the war, Edmund Kirke told us, in the Atlantic Monthly, the story of the life of a brave but unlettered scout, who served in Garfield's army in Southern Kentucky — John Jordan, "from the head of Bayne." * The story, which was a true one, was designed to furnish a sort of running parallel between the lives of two brave and God-fearing men, supposed to be equal in ability, and equally lowly in birth. The one wore the general's epaulets, and still later, as we know, he became President of the United States, known and honored of all men. The other wore the rough homespun garb of the scout, and now that the war is over, he lies in an unknown grave in the Cumberland Mountains. And this difference, so the story tells us, lay in this: "The free schools which Ohio gave the one, and of which Kentucky robbed the other!" "Plant a free school on every Southern cross-road," says Edmund Kirke, "and every Southern Jordan will become a Garfield. Then, and not till then, will the Union be redeemed."

And so this is no idle phrase, "The common school is the hope of our country," and its maintenance is a

* The Bayne is a small tributary of Licking River, in Kentucky.

worthy object which the statesmanship of the people must not neglect. It is something by which all citizens are helped; for in the end all interests are touched by it.

It is too late to ask in America whether this result could be reached in no other way. Private benevolence, private enterprise, the interest of religious bodies,— none of these has been trusted by the American people as a substitute for its own concerted action. In the early history of the West, Judge David D. Banta tells us, ''There were two red rags that required but little shaking to inflame the populace. One of these was sectarianism; the other, aristocracy.'' Our young democracy was in constant fear lest one or the other of these evil influences should enter and dominate its schools.

And even now, while the early prejudices have in great part passed away, our people are especially jealous of any attempt on the part of any organization to turn the schools to its own ends. No church can touch them, and ultimately they are beyond the reach of any political party. Religion, morality, politics even, may be taught in them, but in the interest of religion, morality, and politics alone — not to advance any political party or to increase the following of any religious sect or coalition of sects. In no matter is there greater unanimity of feeling among our people than in this, and he must be an ardent partisan, indeed, who does not feel it and respect it.

From another quarter we hear this objection to popular education: The public schools render the poor discontented with poverty. The child of the common laborer is unwilling to remain common. The pride of Merrie England used to lie in this, that each peasant and workman was contented to be peasant and workman. To those who inherited the good things of the realm, it was a constant pleasure to see the masses below them contented to remain there.

But popular education breaks down the barriers of caste, and therefore increases the restlessness of those shut in by such barriers. The respect for hereditary rank and title is fast disappearing, even in conservative England, to the great dismay of those who have no claim to respect other than that which they had inherited.

Nor has this spirit been wanting in America. My own great-grandfather, John Elderkin Waldo, said in Tolland, Connecticut, a century ago, that there would "never again be good times in New England till the laborer once more was willing to work all day for a sheep's head and pluck." That the good times were past was due, he thought, to the influence of "the little schoolhouses scattered over the hills, which were spreading the spirit of sedition and equality."

But the progress of our country has been along the very lines which this good man so dreaded. The spirit of responsibility fostered by the little schoolhouses has become our surest safeguard against sedition. The man who is intelligent and free has no impulse toward sedition, and for this reason, the people have the right to see that every child shall grow up intelligent and free. They must create their own schools, and they have the plain duty to themselves in making education free to make it likewise compulsory. No child in America has the right to grow up ignorant.

So, leaving the common schools to the State, shall the State's work stop there? Is further education different in its relations to the community? Does a special virtue attach to reading, writing, and arithmetic which is not found in literature, philosophy, history, or science? And shall the State give only the first, and leave the others to shift for themselves?

In Europe, education has progressed from above downward. From the first, higher education has been under public control, and the maintenance of universities is a state duty which few have ever questioned. The struggle for public control in England has concerned only the lower schools, not the universities. The school problem in England to-day is the absurd one of how to make education compulsory without at the same time making it free.

In America the same traditions were inherited, and the founding of the first colleges on a basis of public funds came as a matter of course. The State university, maintained by direct taxation, has been a prominent factor in the organization of each State of the Union outside of the original thirteen, and most of the latter form no exception to the rule. And, with varying fortunes, the growth of each one of these schools has kept pace with the growth of the commonwealth, of which it forms a part.

Eighty years ago, when ignorance and selfishness held less sway in our legislatures than to-day, because the influence of a few men of ideas was proportionately greater, the Constitution of the infant State of Indiana provided that: "Whereas, knowledge and learning generally diffused through a community being essential to the preservation of a free government, and spreading the opportunities and advantages of education through the various parts of the country being highly conducive to this end, it shall be the duty" of the General Assembly to "pass such laws as shall be calculated to encourage intellectual, scientifical and agricultural improvement, by allowing rewards and immunities for the promotion and improvement of arts, sciences, commerce, manufactures, and natural history, and to countenance and encourage the principles of humanity, industry, and morality." To these ends the General Assembly was required "to provide, by law, for a general system of education, ascending in a regular gradation from township schools to a State university, wherein tuition shall be gratis and equally free to all." And all this was guarded by a further provision "for absolute freedom of worship, and that no religious test should ever be required as a qualification to any office of trust or profit," in the State of Indiana.

It is evident from this that the pioneers of the West regarded the colleges as essentially public schools — as much so as the township schools, — and that no idea of separate control and support of the higher institutions was present in their minds. But the judgment of the fathers is ever open to reconsideration. That the last generation thought it wise that the State should provide for higher education is in itself no argument. What shall be our answer in the light of facts to-day? Let us recall the words of Aristotle: "It is the duty of the state to accomplish every worthy end which it can reach better than private effort can do."

I do not need to plead for the value of higher education. The man who doubts this is beyond the reach of argument. The men who have made our country are its educated men; not alone its college graduates — for there is no special virtue in a college diploma,—but men of broad views and high ideals, to give which is the end of higher education.

Moses Coit Tyler, of Cornell University, has said that the men of the early American colleges made success in the Revolutionary War possible. Discussing the effect of the higher institutions of learning on colonial life, he observes: "Still another effect of the early colleges was on the political union and freedom of the colonies. To them we are indebted for American liberty and independence. The colleges educated the people and hastened the advent of freedom by rearing the men who led the colonists in their uprising. It was a contest of brains ten years before the war. The colonies sent to their congresses representatives who began issuing state papers in which the King and Parliament expected to find crude arguments and railings. They were astonished to find in them, however, decency, firmness, and wisdom, solidity, reason, and sagacity. Chatham said: 'You will find nothing like it in the world. The histories of Greece and Rome give us nothing equal to it, and all attempts to force servitude on such a people will be useless.' And these men," continues Mr. Tyler, "were the 'boys' of Harvard, Yale, Princeton, Columbia, and William and Mary."

Dr. Angell has lately said that the history of Iowa is the history of her State university. The greatness of the State has come through the growth of the men the State has trained. If this be true of Iowa, how much more is it true of Michigan, Wisconsin, and Virginia, States which have shown more liberality toward higher education than Iowa has yet done.

"The preliminary education which many of our strongest men have received," says President White, "leaves them simply beasts of prey. It has sharpened their claws and whetted their tusks. A higher education, whether in science, literature, or history, not only sharpens a man's faculties, but gives him new exemplars and ideals. He is lifted to a plane from which he can look down upon success in corruption with the scorn it deserves. The letting-down in character of our National and State councils, has notoriously increased just as the predominance of men of advanced education in those councils has decreased. President Barnard's admirable paper showing the relatively diminishing number of men of advanced education in our public stations, decade by decade, marks no less the rise, decade by decade, of material corruption. This is no mere coincidence. There is a relation here of cause and effect."

The common school is the hope of our country. In like manner, the high school and college are the hope of the common school, and the university the hope of the college. Each part of the system depends on the next higher for its standards and for its inspiration. From those educated in the higher schools the teachers in the lower must come. Lop off the upper branches of the tree, and the sap ceases to rise in its trunk. Cut off the higher schools from the educational system, and its growth and progress stop. Weakness at the head means paralysis of the members.

In the early days, when, as Whittier tells us, "the people sent their wisest men to make the public laws," the close relation of higher education to the public welfare was recognized by all. John Adams said: "It is

to American seminaries of learning that America is indebted for her glory and prosperity.''

The early colleges were sustained, as a matter of course,
either from public funds or from voluntary gifts, in which
every man and woman took part. ''The strongest colleges,'' says Professor Tyler again, ''were not created
by foreign patrons, but by the mass of the people. They
were the children of poverty, self-sacrifice, and toil. Harvard sprang from the popular heart. In its early days,
the families of all the colonies were invited to set apart,
each person, an annual donation for the college, a peck
of corn or twelvepence in money. And to this invita-
tion all responded willingly.''

This direct connection of college and people was one
of constant mutual advantage. It intensified the public
interest in higher education, while it constrained the college to shape its work for the people's good. The high
esteem accorded to the colleges led wealthy men to give
them their attention. So it became with time the fashion
to leave money by bequest to the colleges. In the older
States, such money was usually given to the schools
already established, and, through repeated bequests,
some of these became comparatively wealthy and independent of the aid of the public funds.

In the West and South, this generosity has shown
itself rather in the founding of new institutions, instead
of making the old ones strong. As the little towns of
the forest and prairie grew into great cities, so it was
supposed that, through some hidden force of vitality, the
little colleges would grow into great universities. This
process of planting without watering has gone on until
the whole country is dotted with schools, called by the

name of college or university—on an average more than a dozen to each State. Some of these are well endowed, more ill endowed, and most not endowed at all. But rich or poor, weak or strong, each one serves in some way to perpetuate its founder's ideas and to preserve his name from oblivion.

Many of these are honored names, the names of men who have loved learning and revered wisdom, and who have wished to help, in the only way possible to them, toward the discovery and dissemination of truth. Other names there are which can be honored only when the personality of their possessor is forgotten, men whose highest motive has been to secure a monument, more conspicuous, if not more enduring, than brass. The college founded by rich men, and obliged to depend on the gifts of rich men for its continuance, is sometimes, though not always, forced into degrading positions on account of favors received or favors expected. The officers of more than one of our colleges dare scarcely claim their souls as their own for fear of offending some wealthy patron. There is a college in New England of old and honored name, in which to-day the faculty go about with bated breath for fear of offending two wealthy spinsters in the town, whose money the college hopes to receive.

This growing dependence on the large gifts of a few men tends to carry our colleges farther and farther from the people. A school supported wholly by the interest on endowments too often has little care for public opinion, and hence has little incentive to use its influence toward right opinions. Too often it ceases to respond to the spirit of the times. The *Zeitgeist* passes it by. It becomes the headquarters of conservatism, and within its walls ancient methods and obsolete modes of thought are perpetuated.   Such colleges need what Lincoln called a "bath of the people"—a contact with that humanity for whose improvement the college exists, and which it should be the mission of the college to elevate and inspire. Endowments, independent of popular influence, may become fatal to aggressiveness and to inspiration, however much they may give of material aid to the work of investigation.

It is not a misfortune to a college that it should be dependent on the will of the people it serves.   The pioneer school in the education of women (Mount Holyoke Seminary), has to this day neither patron nor great endowment.   Its founder was a woman, rich only in zeal, who gave all that she had—her life—to the cause of the education of girls.   Mary Lyon's appeal was not to a few rich men to give a hundred thousand apiece, the proceeds of some successful deal in stocks or margins, but to the farmers, clergymen, mechanics, and shopkeepers of New England to give each the little he could spare.   The prayers, and tears, and good wishes, and scanty dollars of thousands of good people gave to this school of faith and hope a most substantial foundation.

Huber says of the University of Oxford, that when it had neither buildings nor land, "its intellectual importance was fully acknowledged."   When it received vast privileges, and vast endowments, its intellectual prominence was obscured by the growth of forms, conventionalities, and sinecures.   It became the stronghold of conservatism, of reaction against modern civilization and modern science.

Darwin speaks of the instruction in the English universities in his time as "incredibly dull," and in almost all of their departments an absolute waste of the student's time. "Half of the professors of Oxford," said a graduate of one of its colleges to me only a few days ago, "live on their stipends and simply soak." The struggle for existence is the basis of progress. Let all the professors in a university be placed beyond the reach of this struggle, and the influence of the university rapidly deteriorates. It is a law of nature, from which nothing can escape. Whatever is alive must show a reason for living.

Not long ago Dr. Döllinger said in the University of Munich that there was not in all America a school which rose to the rank of a third-rate German university. This may be true, so far as privileges and endowments go, for the wolf is close to the door of even our richest colleges. But the usefulness of the college is not gauged by its size, nor by its material equipment. Ernst Haeckel, professor in the third-class University of Jena, tells us that the amount of original investigation actually done in a university is usually in inverse ratio to the completeness and costliness of its equipments. In this paradox there is a basis of truth.

We speak too often of the university and of its powers or needs, as though the school were a separate creature, existing for its own sake. The university exists only in the teachers which compose it and direct its activities. It exists for the benefit of its students, and through them for the benefit of the community, in the extension of culture and the increase in the sum of human knowledge. Its only gain is in making this benefit greater; its only loss is in the diminution or deterioration of its influence. All questions of wealth and equipment are wholly subsidiary to this. The value of the university, then, is not in proportion to its bigness, but to its inspiration. The Good Spirit cares not for the size of its buildings or the length of its list of professors or students. It only asks, in the words of the old reformer, Ulrich von Hütten, if *"die Luft der Freiheit weht?"* — whether "the winds of freedom are blowing."

Doubtless, wealthy men would grade our roads, build our courthouses, conduct our courts — do anything for the public good, — if the State should neglect these matters, or turn them over to private hands. But this would not release the people from their duty in this matter. The people have safety only in independence. "There is," says President White, "no system more unrepublican than that by which a nation or a State, in consideration of a few hundreds or thousands of dollars, delivers over its system of advanced instruction to be controlled and limited by the dogmas and whims of living donors or dead testators. In more than one nation dead hands, stretching out from graves closed generations gone, have lain with a deadly chill upon institutions for advanced instruction during centuries. More than one institution in our own country has felt its grip and chill. If we ought to govern ourselves in anything, it ought to be in this." We should trust the people to judge their own needs, and should have faith that eventually no real need will be left unsatisfied.

But may we not depend upon the interests of some one or more of our religious organizations to furnish the means of higher education? One of our great religious bodies, at least, stands ready to relieve the State of all responsibility for education, higher or lower, if it may be allowed to educate in its own way.   But the people are not willing that this should be so.   They believe that the public school should be free from all sectarian influences of whatever sort.   The other religious bodies in our midst, for the most part, disclaim all desire, as well as all power, to provide for lower education, preferring to spend their strength on the higher.   This is apparently not on account of the superior importance of collegiate education, nor because denominational influences are stronger on young men than on boys.   It is simply because a college is less expensive, and can be more definitely controlled than can a system of lower schools.

I shall have little to say on the subject of denominational colleges, and nothing by way of criticism.   If they do not stand in the way of schools of higher purpose and better equipment, they can do no harm.   If again, like Yale and Harvard, they become transformed into schools of the broadest purpose, they cease to be, whether in name or not, denominational, but become, in fact, schools of the State.   Very many of the denominational schools have been well equipped and well manned, and have fought a good fight for sound learning, as well as for the belief which their founders have deemed correct.   But in too many of them the zeal of the founders has outrun their strength, and a pretense of doing on the part of a few half-starved professors has taken the place of real performance.

It is certainly fair to say this of all the denominational colleges of America: The higher education of youth, pure and simple, is not, cannot be, their chief object. Such schools are founded primarily to promote the growth and preservation of certain religious organizations. This is a worthy object, as all must admit; but this purpose we recognize as something other than simply education.

I read not long ago an appeal from the president of one of our best denominational colleges. Its burden was this: "Unless you are willing to see our church disappear from the West, do not let our college die." This recognizes the ultimate function of the denominational college. The church depends upon it for its educated men. It should furnish the leaders for the church; and the better trained these leaders are, the better for all the people.

But this phase of education is not the State's work; and so no private school or church school can enter the State's scheme of education. To do the State's work, the denominational school must cease to do its own; for no organization can be allowed to color the water in the fountains of popular education. Our bill of rights, the State Constitution, recognizes the equal rights of all men, whatever their religious belief or preferences. This could not be the fact, if the scheme for higher education included sectarian colleges only; and all schools are sectarian in which the ruling body belongs by necessity and by right to some particular religious denomination.

If the State have any duty toward higher education, the existence of denominational colleges does not release it from this duty, any more than the existence of Pinkerton's band of peacemakers absolves the State from its duty to maintain an efficient police system. It is the free investigation and promulgation of truth which is the function of the university. But the denominational school must also stand for the defense of certain doctrines as the

I

ultimate truth.   The highest work demands absolute singleness of purpose.   The school cannot serve two masters; and the school maintained for the special work of the part cannot meet the needs of the whole.

The most unfortunate feature of higher education in America lies in the universal scattering of its educational resources.   For this local pride and denominational zeal are about equally responsible.   If it be true, as Dr. Döllinger says, that among our four hundred American colleges and universities there is not one worthy to rank with the least of the eight maintained by the Kingdom of Prussia, whom have we to thank for this?   Not our poverty, for New York, Pennsylvania, Ohio, and Illinois are not poor, even in comparison with Prussia; not our parsimony, for no people give more freely than we; not our youth, for more than half these schools are older than the great University of Berlin.   It has been this, and this alone — the scattering of educational funds, public and private, at the demand of local ambition or local jealousy.   It has been the creation in each State of a host of little colleges, each one ambitious to control the higher education of its vicinity, and each one more or less definitely standing in the way of any other school which might rise to something better.   Let us take an example:

It was not in response to the educational needs of Kansas that four universities were founded in a single year in one of its real-estate towns, institutions without money and without credit, whose existence can be only one long wail for help from the rich men or rich denominations under whose patronage they are.   There is a little college in the West, almost under the shadow of an excellent State University, which for years sent forth its appeals for help to denominational friends in the East, on the ground that it is the "sole educational oasis" in the great State in which it was located. We have not reached the end of this. The number of our colleges has doubled within the last thirty years, and the increase in number still goes on, far outrunning the rate of improvement in quality.

"Within the last twenty years," said President White in 1874, "I have seen many of these institutions, and I freely confess that my observations have saddened me. Go from one great State to another, and you shall find that this unfortunate system has produced the same miserable results—in the vast majority of our States not a single college or university worthy the name; only a multitude of little schools with pompous names and poor equipments, each doing its best to prevent the establishment of any institution broader and better. The traveler arriving in our great cities generally lands in a railway station costing more than all the university edifices of the State. He sleeps in a hotel in which there is embanked more capital than in the entire university endowment for millions of people. He visits asylums for lunatics, idiots, deaf, dumb, blind,— nay, even for the pauper and criminal,—and finds them palaces. He visits the college buildings for young men of sound mind and earnest purpose, the dearest treasures of the State, and he generally finds them rude barracks.

"Many noble men stand in the faculties of these colleges— men who would do honor to any institution of advanced learning in the world. These men of ours would, under a better system, develop admirably the intellectual treasures of our people and the material resources of our country; but, cramped by want of books, want of apparatus, want of everything needed in advanced instruction, cramped above all by the spirit of this system, very many of them have been paralyzed."

This picture is by no means so dark in the West to-day as it was twenty-five years ago. And the reason for this is to be found in the rise of the State universities. These schools have struggled along with many variations of fortune until within the last few years, when success has come to every one of them, and their development has become the most striking feature in our recent educational history.

When the State universities cast off the self-imposed fetters of the conventional college and took their place with the public schools, supported by the public money and existing for the public good, their real growth began in friends, in numbers, in equipment, in usefulness. What they have deserved they have received, and they will receive in the future. It requires no prophet to foresee that before the middle of the next century these creatures of the public-school system will be the centers of the chief educational forces on our continent. They will cost the people many hundred dollars, perhaps, for every one which is expended now; but every dollar given to higher education shall bring its full return. The greatness of the State is measured not by numbers nor by acres; not by dollars on the tax-roll, but by the wisdom of its people, by the men and women of the State who have learned to take care of themselves.

It is sometimes proposed to treat all higher education simply as a matter of business. Let wisdom be sold in the open market, and let its prices be ruled by the laws of supply and demand. The college professor deals in mental wares, as the shopkeeper deals in material commodities. Let him fill his store with a stock which the people will buy, and advertise what he has, as the shopkeeper does. On this basis he will not carry a dead stock long. There is no room for conservatism in commerce. This is a commercial age, and professors should govern themselves accordingly. If the people want bookkeeping or dancing instead of Latin and Greek, they can have it. If the people retain the old prejudice in favor of classical training, they can have classical courses of the latest Chautauqua pattern, all in English, all the play left in and all the work left out. Busy people can then attend the universities without interruption of their daily work, while the law of supply and demand will regulate everything. Commerce can have no difficulty in modernizing the curriculum. The latest fashions might be quoted in education as well as in millinery.

This could have no result except to cheapen and vulgarize the college. The highest need is not the need of the many; still less is it the multitude's demand. Investigations without immediate pecuniary result would find still less encouragement than now. Vulgarity is the condition of satisfaction with inferior things. A college dependent each day on the day's receipts must pander to vulgarity. And vulgarity, too, is said to be the besetting sin of democracy. If democracy leads to vulgarity, it defeats its own ends. The justification of popular suffrage is to make the multitude better, not to bring the better to the level of the multitude. The many are ready only for the rudiments. The teacher of advanced subjects would starve in open financial competition, while the teacher who could train the many to keep account-books or to get a six-months' license would be exalted. If, on the other hand, the fees of the higher teacher were proportionately increased, only the rich could make use of him, and the rich would find their purposes better served in the endowed schools of other countries.

The demand for many students rather than good ones, already too strong in our colleges, would be intensified, if everything were left to business competition. The whole category of advertising dodges known to the dealers in quack medicines or ready-made clothing would become a permanent part of our higher education. A cheap article furnished at a low price meets with a wonderful sale. We do not need to trust to theory in this matter. In Indiana, Ohio, Illinois, Iowa, and Kansas, are some two-score private schools called colleges. These schools are run without endowment or equipment on the plan of free competition, and for the purpose of making money. One has not to visit many of these to see clearly what would be the result of trusting higher education solely to business enterprise. Any form of educational charity, private gifts, public spirit, denominational zeal, anything leads to better results than this. For the essence of education is something that cannot be bought and sold. It is the inspiration of character, which cannot be rated in our stock exchanges.

If quick sales and steady profits are to be the watchword of educational progress, the student of the future will look toward Lebanon and Valparaiso, rather than toward Johns Hopkins or Harvard, and the great expenditures which New York, and Michigan, and Wisconsin, and California have made for higher education will be a needless waste.

But it is said sometimes that the State cannot properly manage its own institutions. Ignorance and venality are often dominant in public affairs, and it is claimed that work undertaken in the name of the people is sure to be marred by ignorance, affected by partisanship, or tainted by jobbery. The first professor in the State University of Indiana, Baynard R. Hall, said sixty-five years ago: "Nothing, we incline to believe, can ever make State schools and colleges very good ones; but nothing can make them so bad as for Uncle Sam to leave every point open to debate, especially among ignorant, prejudiced, and selfish folks, in a new purchase."

This question touches the very foundation of popular government. In the beginning, as a rule, the affairs of the State are not well administered. Many trials are made. Many blunders are committed before any given piece of work falls into the hands of competent men. But mistakes are a source of education. Sooner or later the right men will be found, and the right management of a public institution will justify itself. What is well done can never be wholly undone. In the long run, few institutions are less subject to partisan influence than a State school. When the foul grip of the spoilsman is once unloosed, it can never be restored. In the evil days which befell the politics of Virginia, when the fair name of the State was traded upon by spoilsmen of every party, of every degree, the one thing in the State never touched by them was the honor of the University of Virginia. And amid all the scandal and disorder which followed our Civil War, what finger of evil has been laid on the Smithsonian Institution or the Military Academy at West Point? On that which is intended for no venal end, the people will tolerate no venal domination. In due time the management of every public institution will be abreast of the highest popular opinion. Sooner or later the wise man leads; for his ability to lead is at once the test and proof of his wisdom.

Charities under public control result badly, not because of the theory, but because of certain relations in practice. Their bad effects tend to increase and perpetuate themselves, because every organization tends to magnify its function; and the sole legitimate function of public charity is to make public charity unnecessary. State schools are not good at first, because under control of unstable forces. They tend to grow better and better; for they tend to draw these forces into a following. All schools tend to improve, because they make their own following. In the same way all charities tend to degenerate, because goodness in this case consists in being needed just as little as possible. Neither schools nor charities are industrial investments, and they are not subject to the laws which govern enterprises for profit.

Methods must be judged by their results. Co-operation in higher education is always legitimate, because those to be educated have not the money which great enterprises cost. Co-operation, on the one hand, and appreciation, on the other, are necessary to build up schools. In similar ways, we must test the best method of carrying out any enterprise. Dr. Amos G. Warner says that if it were found that better results and a better quality of air came from placing the atmosphere in private hands, or using it as a municipal monopoly, he would favor doing so. Matters of this kind cannot be settled by theory, but by experiment.

I need say but a word on the subject of applied education.

Shall the people provide for technical or professional training, as well as for general education? My answer is, Yes; for no other agency will do as well as the State the work that should be done.

Already the General Government has recognized the need of industrial training, and has made liberal provision for it. Special grants of land and money have been made to each State for the purpose of carrying on instruction and investigation in the line of mechanics, engineering and agriculture. Each State has accepted this trust, and in each the work is being carried out with fidelity and with success.

My conclusions may be summed up in a few words:

In every demand the people make, the State must furnish the means for satisfaction. Whatever schools the State may need, the State must create and control.

If the State fails to furnish the means of education, higher or lower, these means will never be adequately furnished. The people must combine to do this work; for in the long run no other agency can do it. Moreover, any other means of support, sooner or later, forms the entering wedge between the schools and the people.

The first constitution of several of our States contained the embodiment of educational wisdom, when it provided for a general system of education, ascending in regular gradation, from the township schools to the State university — free and equal, open to all, and equally open to all forms of religious belief.

The State of California, following the lead of Michigan, did wisely when it added to this the provision for special training in all lines of technical and professional work in which the skill or the wisdom of the individual tends toward the advantage of the community or the State.   Its next duty in this regard is to make this provision adequate, that these professional schools may be capable of doing well what they attempt to accomplish.

VII.

THE HIGHER EDUCATION OF WOMEN.

THE subject of the higher training of young women may resolve itself into three questions:

1. *Shall a girl receive a college education?*

2. *Shall she receive the same kind of a college education as a boy?*

3. *Shall she be educated in the same college?*

As to the first question: It must depend on the character of the girl. Precisely so with the boy. What we should do with either depends on his or her possibilities. No parents should let either boy or girl enter life with any less preparation than the best they can give. It is true that many college graduates, boys and girls alike, do not amount to much after the schools have done the best they can. It is true, as I have elsewhere insisted, that "you cannot fasten a two-thousand-dollar education to a fifty-cent boy,"—or girl either. It is also true that higher education is not alone a question of preparing great men for great things. It must prepare even little men for greater things than they would otherwise have found possible. And so it is with the education of women. The needs of the times are imperative. The highest product of social evolution is the growth of the civilized home — the home that only a wise, cultivated,

123

and high-minded woman can make. To furnish such women is one of the worthiest functions of higher education. No young woman capable of becoming such should be condemned to anything lower. Even with those who are in appearance too dull or too vacillating to reach any high ideal of wisdom, this may be said — it does no harm to try. A few hundred dollars is not much to spend on an experiment of such moment. Four of the best years of one's life spent in the company of noble thoughts and high ideals cannot fail to leave their impress. To be wise, and at the same time womanly, is to wield a tremendous influence, which may be felt for good in the lives of generations to come. It is not forms of government by which men are made or unmade. It is the character and influence of their mothers and their wives. The higher education of women means more for the future than all conceivable legislative reforms. And its influence does not stop with the home. It means higher standards of manhood, greater thoroughness of training, and the coming of better men. Therefore, let us educate our girls as well as our boys. A generous education should be the birthright of every daughter of the republic as well as of every son.

2. *Shall we give our girls the same education as our boys?* Yes, and no. If we mean by the *same* an equal degree of breadth and thoroughness, an equal fitness for high thinking and wise acting, yes, let it be the same. If we mean this: Shall we reach this end by exactly the *same* course of studies? then my answer must be, No. For the same course of study will not yield the same results with different persons. The ordinary "college

course" which has been handed down from generation to generation is purely conventional. It is a result of a series of compromises in trying to fit the traditional education of clergymen and gentlemen to the needs of men of a different social era. The old college course met the needs of nobody, and therefore was adapted to all alike. The great educational awakening of the last twenty years in America has lain in breaking the bonds of this old system. The essence of the new education is individualism. Its purpose is to give to each young man that training which will make a man of *him*. Not the training which a century or two ago helped to civilize the mass of boys of that time, but that which will civilize this particular boy. One reason why the college students of 1895 are ten to one in number as compared with those of 1875, is that the college training now given is valuable to ten times as many men as could be reached or helped by the narrow courses of twenty years ago.

In the university of to-day the largest liberty of choice in study is given to the student. The professor advises, the student chooses, and the flexibility of the courses makes it possible for every form of talent to receive proper culture. Because the college of to-day helps ten times as many men as that of yesterday could hope to reach, it is ten times as valuable. This difference lies in the development of special lines of work and in the growth of the elective system. The power of choice carries the duty of choosing rightly. The ability to choose has made a man out of the college boy and transferred college work from an alternation of tasks and play to its proper relation to the business of life. Meanwhile the old ideals have not risen in value. If our colleges were to go back to the cut-straw of medievalism, to their work of twenty years ago, their professors would speak to empty benches. In those colleges which still cling to these traditions the benches are empty to-day — or filled with idlers, which to a college is a fate worse than death.

The best education for a young woman is surely not that which has proved unfit for the young man. She is an individual as well as he, and her work gains as much as his by relating it to her life. But an institution which meets the varied needs of varied men can also meet the varied needs of the varied women. The intellectual needs of the two classes are not very different in many important respects. The special or professional needs, so far as they are different, will bring their own satisfaction. Those who have had to do with the higher training of women know that the severest demands can be met by them as well as by men. There is no demand for easy or "goody-goody" courses of study for women except as this demand has been encouraged by men. In this matter the supply has always preceded the demand.

There are, of course, certain average differences between men and women as students. Women have often greater sympathy or greater readiness of memory or apprehension, greater fondness for technique. In the languages and literature, often in mathematics and history, they are found to excel. They lack, on the whole, originality. They are not attracted by unsolved problems and in the inductive or "inexact" sciences, they seldom take the lead. The "motor" side of their minds and natures is not strongly developed. They do not work for results as much as for the pleasure of study.

In the traditional courses of study — traditional for men — they are often very successful. Not that these courses have a fitness for women, but that women are more docile and less critical as to the purposes of education. And to all these statements there are many exceptions. In this, however, those who have taught both men and women must agree; the training of women is just as serious and just as important as the training of men, and no training is adequate for either which falls short of the best.

3. *Shall women be taught in the same classes as men?* This is partly a matter of taste. It does no harm whatever to either men or women to meet those of the other sex in the same classrooms. But if they prefer not to do so, let them do otherwise. Considerable has been said for and against the union in one institution of technical schools and schools of liberal arts. The technical quality is emphasized by its separation from general culture. But I believe better men are made where the two are not separated. The culture studies and their students gain from the feeling of reality and utility cultivated by technical work. The technical students gain from association with men and influences of which the aggregate tendency is toward greater breadth of sympathy and a higher point of view.

A woman's college is more or less distinctly a technical school. In most cases, its purpose is distinctly stated to be such. It is a school of training for the profession of womanhood. It encourages womanliness of thought as more or less different from the plain thinking which is called manly. The brightest work in women's colleges is often accompanied by a nervous strain, as though its doer were fearful of falling short of some outside standard. The best work of men is natural, is unconscious, the normal result of the contact of the mind with the problem in question.

In this direction, I think, lies the strongest argument for co-education. This argument is especially cogent in institutions in which the individuality of the student is recognized and respected. In such schools each man, by his relation to action and realities, becomes a teacher of women in these regards, as, in other ways, each cultivated woman is a teacher of men.

In woman's education, as planned for women alone, the tendency is toward the study of beauty and order. Literature and language take precedence over science. Expression is valued more highly than action. In carrying this to an extreme, the necessary relation of thought to action becomes obscured. The scholarship developed is ineffective, because it is not related to success. The educated woman is likely to master technique, rather than art; method, rather than substance. She may know a good deal, but she can do nothing. Often her views of life must undergo painful changes before she can find her place in the world.

In schools for men alone, the reverse condition often obtains. The sense of reality obscures the elements of beauty and fitness. It is of great advantage to both men and women to meet on a plane of equality in education. Women are brought into contact with men who can do things — men in whom the sense of reality is strong, and who have definite views in life. This influence effects them for good. It turns them away from sentimentalism. It is opposed to the unwholesome state of mind called "monogamic marriage." It gives tone to their religious thoughts and impulses. Above all, it tends to encourage action as governed by ideals, as opposed to that resting on caprice. It gives them better standards of what is possible and impossible when the responsibility for action is thrown upon them.

In like manner, the association with wise, sane, and healthy women has its value for young men. This value has never been fully realized, even by the strongest advocates of co-education. It raises their ideal of womanhood, and the highest manhood must be associated with such an ideal. This fact shows itself in many ways; but to point out its existence must suffice for the present paper.

At the present time, the demand for the higher education of women is met in three different ways:

1. In separate colleges for women, with courses of study more or less parallel with those given in colleges for men. In some of these the teachers are all women, in some mostly men, and in others a more or less equal division obtains. In nearly all of these institutions, those old traditions of education and discipline are more prevalent than in colleges for men, and nearly all retain some trace of religious or denominational control. In all, the *Zeitgeist* is producing more or less commotion, and the changes in their evolution are running parallel with those in colleges for men.

2. In annexes for women to colleges for men. In these, part of the instruction given to the men is repeated for the women, though in different classes or rooms, and there is more or less opportunity to use the same libra-

J

ries and museums.   In some other institutions, the relations are closer, the privileges of study being similar, the difference being mainly in the rules of conduct by which the young women are hedged in, the young men making their own.

It seems to me that the annex system cannot be a permanent one.   The annex student does not get the best of the institution, and the best is none too good for her. Sooner or later she will demand it, or go where the best can be found.   The best students will cease to go to the annex.   The institution must then admit women on equal terms, or not admit them at all.   There is certainly no educational reason why a woman should prefer the annex of one institution when another equally good throws its doors wide open for her.

3. The third system is that of co-education.   In this system young men and young women are admitted to the same classes, subjected to the same requirements, and governed by the same rules.   This system is now fully established in the State institutions of the North and West, and in most other colleges in the same region. Its effectiveness has long since passed beyond question among those familiar with its operation.   Other things being equal, the young men are more earnest, better in manners and morals, and in all ways more civilized than under monastic conditions.   The women do more work in a more natural way, with better perspective and with saner incentives than when isolated from the influence and society of men.   There is less of silliness and folly where a man is not a novelty.   In co-educational institutions of high standards, frivolous conduct or scandals of any form are unknown.   The responsibility for

decorum is thrown from the school to the woman, and the woman rises to the responsibility. Many professors have entered Western colleges with strong prejudices against co-education. These prejudices have never endured the test of experience. What is well done has a tonic effect on the mind and character. The college girl has long since ceased to expect any particular leniency because she is a girl. She stands or falls with the character of her work.

It is not true that the character of college work has been in any way lowered by co-education. The reverse is decidedly the case. It is true that untimely zeal of one sort or another has filled the West with a host of so-called colleges. It is true that most of these are weak and doing poor work in poor ways. It is true that most of these are co-educational. It is also true that the great majority of their students are not of college grade at all. In such schools, low standards rule, both as to scholarship and as to manners. The student fresh from the country, with no preparatory training, will bring the manners of his home. These are not always good manners, as manners are judged. But none of these defects are derived from co-education; nor are any of these conditions in any way made worse by it.

A final question: Does not co-education lead to marriage? Most certainly it does; and this fact need not be and cannot be denied. But such marriages are not usually premature. It is certainly true that no better marriages can be made than those founded on common interests and intellectual friendships.

A college man who has known college women is not drawn to those of lower ideals and inferior training. His choice is likely to be led toward the best he has known. A college woman is not led by propinquity to accept the attentions of inferior men.

I have before me the statistics of the faculty of a university open to both sexes alike. Of the eighty professors and instructors, twenty-seven men and women are still unmarried. Of the remaining fifty-three, twenty-one have taken the Bachelor's degree in co-educational institutions, and have married college associates; twelve, mostly from colleges not co-educational, have married women from other colleges, and in twenty cases the wives are not college graduates.

It will be seen, then, that nearly all those who are graduates of co-educational colleges have married college friends. In most cases college men have chosen college women; and in all cases both men and women are thoroughly satisfied with the outcome of co-education. It is part of the legitimate function of higher education to prepare women, as well as men, for happy and successful lives.

An Eastern professor, lately visiting a Western State university, asked one of the seniors what he thought of the question of co-education.

"I beg your pardon," said the student; "what question do you mean?"

"Why, co-education," said the professor; "the education of women in colleges for men."

"Oh," said the student, "co-education is not a question here."

And he was right. Co-education is never a question where it has been fairly tried.

VIII.

THE TRAINING OF THE PHYSICIAN.*

IT is a matter of common observation that the various elements in the educational fabric of America are not in any proper sense parts of an educational system. Each kind of school has developed in its own way, in response to a special demand, or in furtherance of some educational tradition. Our colleges are English in blood and ancestry, our universities German. Our academies are children of the colleges, and our high schools and professional schools are for the most part wholly distinct in their origin and native to our soil. They have arisen in obedience to the law of supply and demand, and their methods and ideals are often wholly at variance with those of the colleges.

There have been some good results arising from these conditions. The progress of evolution is most rapid where the chains of tradition are weakest. These chains have been strongest in our colleges; and of all our schools our colleges have been until lately the least progressive. The chains of tradition have been weakest in our professional schools; but all that they have gained in freedom has been more than lost by their separation from other educational agencies. The bad results of our lack of correlation have been numerous and positive. Among these have been the general weakness of the whole sys-

* Commencement address at Cooper Medical College, San Francisco, 1892; reprinted from Occidental Medical Times, January, 1893.

tem and a prodigious waste of strength throughout its parts.   Much of the best of the educational thought of the day is devoted to the work of bringing together and properly dovetailing the scattered parts of our system. To consider a single one of these problems, the relation of medical education to the college education, is the purpose of the present paper.

The Bachelor's degree, as generally understood, is an index of general culture, the mark of that degree of training which fairly prepares a bright man to enter upon professional work.   The colleges have, as a rule, regarded this standard as a low one, rather than a high one, and with the improvement of our educational methods, the requirements for this degree have been steadily advanced. Better work and more of it is necessary for graduation with each succeeding class.   The result of this is, that the student who has spent all his life in the schools is not through college and ready to begin his professional studies much before the age of twenty-two, while the man who is forced by any reason to interrupt his school work may be anywhere from twenty-five to thirty years of age on graduation.

This fact has led to a demand for the shortening of the college course in the interests of practical life.   The medical faculty of Harvard University has led in this demand in the interest of professional studies, and the question of reducing the college course from four years to three, has become a subject of general discussion.   It is, of course, evident that there is no special virtue in four years of work, as opposed to three, or to five, or to any other particular number; nor is there any universal agreement at present as to the separation of the work of the colleges from that of the high school or academy. That the standard of requirement for admission at Harvard is unusually high may be in itself a valid reason for lowering the requirements for graduation in Harvard. In that case, however, the discussion of the question would practically concern Harvard University alone.

But viewing the subject from the side of the student of medicine, this question is before us: Is the college course too long? That it is so, is practically the verdict of the medical schools as well as of the great body of physicians themselves. The medical colleges have made the preliminary training a matter of luxury, rather than of necessity, by putting into the same classes, under the same instruction, the graduates of colleges and persons who come from the country district school. If general culture be essential to professional success, the medical college should say so to those who enter its doors. So far as any official action in most of our medical colleges is concerned, the illiterate boor, if he can sign the matriculation book, is as ready for medical education as the most accomplished college graduate.

The physicians of our country say the same thing; for the number of college-bred men in medicine is lower than in almost any other profession. Statistics furnished me by Professor Richard G. Boone, show that in the United States at present, about one clergyman in four, one lawyer in five, and one physician in twelve, has had a college education. Connected with the lack of preparatory training on the part of medical students, there are certain recognized facts, one of which is this: Taking the country over, of all classes of students, those in medicine are as a rule (though such a rule admits of many individual exceptions) the most reckless in their mode of life and the most careless of the laws of hygiene, and of decencies in general, of any class of students whatsoever. This is not so true now as it was a few years ago. For this change the rising standards of our medical schools are certainly responsible. This change results directly from making it more difficult for uncultivated men to win the Doctor's degree, and indirectly from bringing better men into the field as competitors. Already there is a good deal of crowding at the bottom of the stairs in the profession; and in view of this fact the scramble for the name of doctor is somewhat abating.

A concerted effort is now being made to raise the standard of the profession of medicine by raising the general culture of physicians. Its purpose is to make medicine a worthy branch of applied science, and its votaries men to whom the word *Science* is not an empty name. It has been a frequent reproach to the medical profession that physicians are not doing their part in this age of scientific investigation and discovery, in a time when the boundaries of knowledge are widening in every direction at a rate of progress never before known.

It is said that, although their work brings them into daily contact with the very subjects over which the battles of science are being waged, they know nothing of the struggle and have no share in the victory. Right in the path of the physician lie the great problems of the nature of heredity, of psychology, histology, sociology, criminology — the manifold problems of all the laws of life. Individual physicians have found out many things — much more than the world outside has recognized; but the profession at large is not interested in these matters. Although not one of these problems is alien to the daily work of any physician, the average practitioner neither knows what is already known nor what is yet to be found out.

When our physicians are ready for it, the whole administration of criminal law will be turned over to them. The responsibility for crime or craziness cannot be fixed by jurisprudence. The criminal cannot be cured by law, and no good end is served by the punishments the law metes out. He can perhaps be healed. If incurable, he can be kept in confinement; and to physicians, and to them alone, the community must look for help in these matters.

If our physicians be deficient in general culture, and if it be true that they are not taking their share in the progress of science, may not these facts be associated? May we not have here the relation of cause and effect? What then is the remedy? Is it not this? Bring in better men; shut out from the medical profession the ignorant, the trifling, and the unambitious, the tinker and the job-worker, and reserve the training of our medical schools for those who can bring to their work the instincts, the traditions, and the outlook of the scholar.

A writer has lately maintained that a man without independent means should not study medicine. The physician can no longer be sure of earning his living in our cities on account of the competition of the free dispensaries. Whether the free dispensary be a wise charity or not, is perhaps an open question. But surely the skillful physician has a field which the free dispensary cannot invade. The physician we dream of is something more than the automatic dispenser of drugs. Skill and wis-

dom will always be valued and paid for. The thoroughly
trained man fears no competition; for it is by measurement with others that his value can be estimated.

For the training which shall enable the medical student
to enter on his professional work in the spirit of science
and of scholarship, we must look to the college. To give
this breadth and skill, to fit men and women to enter
with large views and trained minds on the work of life,
the college exists. The general culture of the physician
should have its roots in the work of the college. The
amount and the kind of culture regarded by the colleges
in general as essential to the highest professional success,
they have roughly estimated by their requirements for
the degree of Bachelor of Arts. This degree, or its equivalent, has been taken by the American Academy of Medicine as its standard of admission to membership. Some
measure of culture is better than no measure, however
fluctuating the standard may be, and this is the only measure which is furnished by the colleges themselves. If
we require or recognize collegiate attainments at all, the
Bachelor's degree furnishes the only available method
by which general culture may be indicated.

It is very easy to see that this standard is not absolute;
that it means in one college something different in kind
as well as in amount from that which obtains in another.
Its meaning to-day is not what it was ten years ago, nor
what it will be ten years hence. Much time has been
spent in tabulating the different elements involved in the
requirements for this degree in the different American
colleges. The results are unsatisfactory; for the value
of the degree is not to be determined by the percentage
of required work in Greek, Latin, German, nor in any

of the sciences. The school which shows the greatest amount of required work in any particular subject may be the very one where the least of this work is really done. The freedom of the elective system gives, in any line of work, the greatest possibilities. But the very fact of freedom prevents its results from appearing in a table of percentages. The essential fact is the extent to which the spirit of the scholar has been inspired in the student, and this varies in every case with the differences of teacher and scholar. So this fluctuation is inherent in the nature of things. It is well that it should be so, and that its variations should be greater, rather than less, for its maximum indicates the unrestrained influence of great teachers. There are men in some of our colleges under whom a single year's study is better than many years of ordinary drill.

Moreover, America is a broad land, and yields nourishment for many different educational ideas. In many cases, too, the variations in the requirements for a degree are more apparent than real; for the difference of subjects pursued in a college course is a very small matter as compared with the question whether the best years of youth are spent in mental training, in the demands of trade, or in fruitless idleness.

Is this standard of the Bachelor's degree too high for the best results in professional work? In other words, is the physician who has waited to secure his Bachelor's degree thereby handicapped in his professional life? Has he lost a year or two which, in this hurrying age, he can never regain? I cannot think so, and I am sure no such view could be sustained by statisics. Are the members of the American Academy less successful than their brother physicians? Is the college degree which they bear the mark of those who have fallen behind in the active work of the physician? To state this question is to answer it. The broadest outlook on nature and human life goes with the highest professional success. The educated physician is the man of science. The uneducated physician is the quack.

But, as I have said, our medical schools seem to think otherwise; for in most of them the requirement for entrance, so far from being that of college graduation, is far less than that necessary even for entrance into the college. If general training be important, the schools should insist upon it. That it is not necessary in their judgment is apparently shown by the requirements for admission.

This condition of things, I believe, has two causes — the one discreditable to the profession, the other to the colleges. In the first place, most of our medical schools are scantily endowed, or else are purely private ventures. It has been for them a business necessity to demand not the preparation they want, but that which they can get. In other words, they have been forced to cater to the desire of ignorance and impatience to take part in the honor and emoluments of the medical profession. For the same reason the standard of graduation has been kept low. A high standard would diminish the sale of the lecture tickets. The character of the profession has been lowered that the medical college may be self-supporting; for not to support itself in part at least means to close its doors.

I do not mean to depreciate this class of medical schools; for many of our best teachers of medicine have belonged to them, and have given their instruction in the intervals of an active practice. But this is not the ideal medical school; for no school can be effective until it exists for its work alone—instruction and investigation, with no ulterior end whatever. Its teachers should never have to look to the interests of the cash account, and its examiners should never be forced to say that black is white at the demand of an empty treasury. The medical schools of the future will be sustained as necessary parts of university work, and the freedom of the university professor will be the right of the teacher of medicine. The medical schools have the same claim for support that other professional schools should have. They have the same claim on the interests of the wealthy friends of education. In the West and in the South, where colleges and the lower schools are alike maintained at the public expense, the medical schools have the same claim for State support that is awarded to other parts of the public-school system.

When a medical school is well endowed, or has the State behind it, it can exact the standards the good of the profession requires. Till then it is at the mercy of the demands about it. Its students are the product of its surroundings, not the choice of the school itself.

That the proper training of teachers is a matter of real economy has been recognized by every State in the Union, and this fact has led to the establishment of the State normal schools. We recognize that thorough professional training is the best antidote to educational quackery and fraud. It is cheaper for the people to pay for the education of the teachers, and then to pay the teachers an increased salary because they are educated, than it is to depend on the haphazard training furnished by the law of supply and demand.

There was a time when to be fit for nothing else was the chief requisite for the schoolmaster. But experience has shown that such teaching is the costliest of all. It has shown that one teacher worth two hundred dollars a month is more effective for educational advancement than ten who find their proper level at forty or fifty.

As with teaching, so with all other professions — cheap work is never good. It is often said in the West, and this statement is applauded by our farmers and mechanics, the very men who should know better, that the State should not support schools for the making of physicians and lawyers. The people should not be taxed to help young men into these easy professions already so overcrowded.

Let us state this proposition in another form: Shall the State demand that the lawyers, physicians, surveyors, and architects who serve its people should know their business? Why not? Have we not had enough of the work of frauds and fools? The money wasted each year in California on quacks and quack medicines, revealed remedies, and blessed handkerchiefs, would educate every physician in the State who has the brains to bear education.

Bring in better men. There is no more effective way of thinning out incompetent men in any profession than to bring trained men in competition with them. If the State could require each physician or lawyer to know what a physician or lawyer ought to know, the quacks and pettifoggers would disappear as surely as an army of tramps before a stone-pile. This country is now their paradise. These professions are overcrowded in America simply because they are not professions at all.

Not long ago the University of Berlin refused to recognize the degree of Doctor of Medicine from an American school as a degree at all. It is easy to see a reason for this. In our best schools the total educational requirement for this degree is lower than in Berlin. In our worst schools it may fall seven years behind. One of the very best of our medical colleges has lately decided to raise the standard of admission a little each year until 1899. When this is done the entrance requirements will be those of the Freshman class in the Academic department of the same institution.

American physicians are often among the most skillful in the world; but this comes through individual capacity and through that native ingenuity with which every American is blest, rather than from any requirement of the schools.

It was my fortune some three years ago to meet that which in Europe is regarded as a typical American physician — one who was taught by nature, and not by the schools. He was, therefore, regarded by the people of rural England with a reverence which the man of training often fails to inspire. It was in the solemn and decorous village of Stratford-on-Avon that I met this physician. Riding on a gilded circus wagon drawn by four noble horses, attired in a cowboy's splendid uniform, in gray *sombrero*, with a red *serape*, accompanied by a band of musicians dressed as cowboys and stained as Indians, this man was going through England selling from the wagon that famous remedy of the Kickapoo Indians, the August Flower. It cures every disease known to that countryside by the simple purification of the blood.   In one day in Stratford-on-Avon he won back for America all the money the Americans have spent on the shrine of Shakspeare within the past three hundred years; and on Sunday evening I saw him installed in the famous parlors in the ancient Red Horse Inn at Stratford, sacred to the memory of Washington Irving, as the one American there worthy to dine within its historic walls.   The scarcity of quacks in England made his business profitable.

A medical student killed himself in New York the other day, leaving behind him these words: "I die because there is room for no more doctors." Over-crowded, poor fellow, smothered by the weight of the mass of his fellow-incompetents, and all this while the science of medicine stands on the verge of the greatest discoveries since the time of Galen and Æsculapius. "Room for no more doctors," just now when the theory of evolution begins to throw its electric light down thousands of avenues closed to the fathers of medicine; "room for no more doctors," when the germ theory is working its revolution in surgery, obstetrics, and in the treatment of contagious diseases; "room for no more doctors," when a thousand applications of antiseptics and anesthetics are yet to be made, or made in better ways; "no more doctors," when with the discoveries of each succeeding year it is more and more worth while to be a doctor — for each year strengthens the doctor's grip on the forces of sin and death.

There is always a place for doctors; but only for men of the nobler sort.   Their profession is not overcrowded. The overcrowd is outside the profession.   The great majority of our physicians have had only the commonest of school advantages. What wonder that so much of the world is a sealed book to them? Men who do not read "bound books," cannot share in the advancement of science.

I do not mean to depreciate in any way the work of the many who are really great in the noblest of all professions. Of our best we have the right to be proud. It is only when we regard the amount of ignorant, empirical, and dishonest work called professional that the record grows dark, and we doubt whether our American system of medical *laissez-faire* can be a wise one.

Only by the requirement of training can our professions be restored to their ancient respectability. Their work must rest on a basis of science. A man who has spent years with the great jurists will not sell his soul for a twenty-five dollar fee to the first scoundrel who would use him. The scientific physician does not prostitute his skill in any of the hundred ways condemned by the code of ethics. A true man cannot be used for base purposes. *Noblesse oblige;* and professional training implies professional honor. Only the highest standards can purge the profession of parasites and quacks; only honest knowledge can save us from the Christian scientist and the almanac. But in every demand the people make the State must furnish the means for satisfaction.

As I have already said, there has been another reason why the medical student has shunned the college, namely, the tremendous waste involved in the old-fashioned, prescribed course; or, for that matter, in any course of study inflexibly prearranged. This waste is threefold.

K

The time spent on subjects in no wise concerned with the future studies of the student — thoughts which form no part of his culture; second, the time spent on subjects for which the student has no aptitude, from which he derives not the strength gained by mastery, but only the aversion felt for the unwelcome task; and third, and greatest of all, the waste of subjects taught by dull teachers, dry, dreary, or mechanical, from whom the student received nothing, because there was nothing in them to give.

Those of us who have been through the prescribed course of the college have run the gauntlet of all these parasites on higher education. Only he who is familiar with the life of college boys can realize the great waste connected with work in wrong subjects under wrong teachers; and no one can estimate the number who have been repelled from the college by one or both of these evil influences. Many of those who remained to the end did so because their college lives were spent in the atmosphere of good-fellowship, not because they were attracted by their teachers or the work they were set to do

If our medical schools cede four years to the culture of the colleges, they have the right to ask that the colleges waste no time. They cannot ask any particular curriculum or any special order of studies. They can only ask for the student the freedom of choice which shall enable him to steer clear of deficient teachers, and to work in fields from which he may in later life expect to reap a harvest. The college should furnish such means of study that the future student shall not go to the medical school ignorant of the use of the scalpel and the microscope. Cats are abundant and cheap. The elementary facts of anatomy can be learned from them in college far better than in the dissecting-room of the special school, where advanced work should be done, instead of the bungling efforts of beginners who do not know a vein from a tendon.

The college course should also teach the medical student the general facts and theory of chemistry and the processes of chemical manipulation. The elements of botany and of vegetable and animal physiology should be in his possession; the facts of comparative anatomy, and the great laws of life, of natural selection, heredity, variability, functional activity, and response to external stimulus, which form the basis of organic evolution. He should know a bacterium when he sees it, and should know how to see it. He should have heard of the correlation and conservation of forces; in short, he should know what is meant by scientific investigation, and in some degree have caught the inspiration of it. The physician should, moreover, learn to write and speak good English. Besides this, he ought to — he *must* — read French and German. Other languages will not hurt him, nor will a knowledge of literature, philosophy, or history.

Such a course of study as is here contemplated is actually provided in the undergraduate department of several of our universities. It is, however, a course of general culture, not a technical or professional course. This course, or its equivalent, is recognized as a necessary condition of entrance in the new medical school of Johns Hopkins University. No more important movement has been taken toward raising the standard of medical education in America than this recognition by Johns Hopkins University of the absolute necessity of mental culture as a requisite for professional training.

But all that he wants the student cannot get in a four years' college course, no matter how fully he may crowd it. The whole time is little enough if every moment be saved. But four years is far too long if it is made a time for dawdling and cramming, and for merely going through the motions of study. Let the college permit the medical student to get a fair return for every hour he spends, and the requirement of a college degree at the door of the medical school will shut out no worthy man, nor will it hold back any in the race for life.

Nor need the medical school fear that it will suffer through the neglect of the college to furnish the necessary training. Let the collegiate course be required as a requisite to the professional degree, and the inexorable law of the survival of the fittest will eliminate every waste teacher and every waste subject from the college course for the student preparing for work in medicine.

But I do not wish to lay a disproportionate stress upon the college diploma. It is at the best a temporary thing — a mere milestone, convenient to measure from so long as it is in sight. The world, it has been said, "cares little for that baby badge," though it will never cease to care for the culture that ought to be behind it.

Some day, our students will need the badge no longer; and the Bachelor's degree, with college honors, and prizes, and other playthings of our educational childhood will be laid aside. All these things are forms, and forms only, and our higher education is fast outgrowing them. The boundary line between general and professional education will be broken down to the advantage of both. We shall have the "school where any person can have instruction in any study," and the study of the humanities need not end where the study of the human body is begun. Let each come who will, and let each take what he can, and let the ideals be so high that no one will imagine that he is getting where he is not. Scholars can be made neither by driving nor by coaxing. In any profession the inspiration and the example of educated men is the best surety that the generation which succeeds them shall be likewise men of culture.

IX

LAW SCHOOLS AND LAWYERS.*

MR. JAMES BRYCE, writing of the universities of America, uses these words: "While, of all the institutions of the country, they are those of which the Americans speak most modestly, and, indeed, deprecatingly, they are those which seem to be at this very moment making the swiftest progress, and to have the best promise for the future. They are supplying exactly those things which European critics have hitherto found lacking in America, and they are contributing to her political as well as to her contemplative life elements of inestimable worth."

The various influences — German, English, and American — which are molding our higher education, are joining together to produce the American university. And, as Mr. Bryce has clearly indicated, the American university is becoming an institution in every way worthy of our great republic. Its swaddling-clothes of English tradition are being cast aside, and it is growing to be American in the high sense of adjustment to the American people's needs. The academic work of the best American institutions is characterized by vigor and thoroughness, and in the free air that pervades them there is every promise for their future.

But with all this, the professional schools of America

* Published in The Forum, 1895.

have not taken their part in the university development. It has been lately said of the American law schools, for example, that they are the weakest, and therefore the worst, to be found in any civilized country. Broadly speaking, and taking out some half-dozen notable exceptions (not so many nor so notable as they should be), this statement cannot be denied. Of this deficiency, its causes and its remedy, I propose briefly to treat in this paper.

In Europe, professional training is in general the culmination of university education. It is not so in America. It is here rather a "practical short-cut," by which uneducated or ineducable men are helped to the rewards of knowledge and skill with the least possible loss of time. In most of our States provision is made for a system of public education beginning with the common schools and culminating in the university. The law schools, however, in the different States form no part of this system. They are rarely, even, in real alliance with it. Their place is with the "independent normal" and the "school of oratory." Instead of a requirement of general intelligence and a special knowledge of economics, history, literature, and language, as a preparation for the study of law, our law schools have been eager to admit any one who can pay the required fees and perchance read the English language.

Instead of trained professors who make the methods of investigation and instruction in law the work of a lifetime, we find in most of our law schools lawyers who have turned incidentally to teaching, with no knowledge of the methods by which teaching may be made effective. Some of them are young men who have not yet found anything more serious to do. But usually the chairs of law are occupied by broken-down lawyers, released from active practice — old men who read old lectures to audiences inattentive or occupied with newspapers, or who conduct a lifeless quiz from lifeless text-books. Sometimes these veterans of a thousand fields are wise with the results of many experiences. These teachers may interest and inspire their students. But training they seldom give. Only the man with whom teaching is the first interest can be an effective teacher. Able jurists sometimes fill these chairs, men still in active practice, whose hour in the classroom is taken early in the morning or late in the afternoon, before or after the arduous duties of a day in court. With these men the court, and not the school, occupies their thought and fills their ambitions.

The law students are in general assistants in law offices or clerks in business establishments. They devote their hours outside the classroom, not to library research or to the investigations of principles and precedents, but to the making of money. The law school is expected not to interrupt their usual vocations. The atmosphere of culture which surrounds every real institution of learning, and which it is the business of great teachers to create, is unknown to the average student of law.

Often the law school appears in its register as a branch of some university. In most such cases this relation is one which exists only in name. It is a common expression that such and such a college is "surrounded by a fringe of professional schools." These exist as stolons or suckers around a stalk of corn, rather than as representing "the full corn in the ear." When a nominal

alliance exists, it rests not often on unity of purpose or
method, but on the fact of mutual service.   The reputation of the university tends to advertise the law school.
The roll of law students swells the apparent attendance
of the university.   By the number of names on the
register the success of the American university is popu-
larly measured.

There is, besides, a strong force of precedent, which
causes each new law school to be modeled on the lines
of the old ones.   These influences, and others, oblige
our universities to wink at the obvious incongruity of the
requirement of elaborate and careful preparation for the
study of literature, chemistry, and economics, while for
the study of law a mere reading acquaintance with the
English language passes as adequate.   More than once
college faculties in this matter have had to subordinate
their opinions to those of timid boards of trustees, who
are afraid that high standards in a law school would be
fatal to its success, measuring success in the conventional
fashion, as boards of trustees are prone to do.

It is thus true, as President Eliot has said, that into an
American law school any man "can walk from the
street."   But in most of the States he can do better, or
worse, than this.   From the street he can walk directly
into the profession of law, disregarding even the formulas
of matriculation or graduation.   Even the existence of
the law school is a concession to educational tradition.
It is possible with us to enter any one of the "learned
professions" with no learning whatsoever.   In fact, in
many of our States it requires no more preparation to
be admitted to the bar than to be admitted to the saw-
buck.   Fortunately, admission to either on these terms

carries with it no prestige or social elevation whatever. But the danger in the one case is greater than in the other. The inefficient lawyer may work the ruin of interests intrusted to him. The ignorant physician is more dangerous than the plague. The incompetent wood-sawyer harms only the wood-pile. A large part of our criminal records is devoted to legal and medical malpractice. In other words, our bulk of crime is swollen by robbery and murder committed under the guise of professional assistance. When the professions cease to be open wide to adventurers and thieves, they will rise to something of their ancestral dignity. It has been said that the only "learned profession" in America at present is that of engineer. The value of knowledge and training in the various applications of science to human affairs has always been recognized among us. The people have freely taxed themselves for industrial instruction, and it is now generally recognized as a necessary part of the State university system. The faculty in mechanic arts stands on an equality with the university faculties, and in general the standards of admission and methods of work in these branches compare favorably with those in any other field. The reason for this is not far to seek. The necessity of education in these lines is self-evident. Men cannot trifle with the forces of nature. The incompetence, or ignorance, or dishonesty of an engineer will soon make itself evident. The incompetence of men in other professions is not less disastrous, but it is more easily concealed. And for this reason the common man regards it with greater indifference.

It seems to me that the essential weakness of the American law school, as well as that of our professional schools in general, lies in the method of organization. They have lost their place in the university. In a recent address,* Professor James Bradley Thayer has these strong words:

"We must not be content with a mere lip service, with merely tagging our law schools with the name of a university, while they lack entirely the university spirit and character. What, then, does our undertaking involve, and what that conception of the study of our English system of law, which, in Blackstone's phrase, 'extends the pomœria of university learning, and adopts this new tribe of citizens within these philosophical walls'? It means this: that our law must be studied and taught as other great sciences are taught at the universities, as deeply, by like methods, and with a concentration and lifelong devotion of all the powers of a learned and studious faculty. If our law be not a science worthy, and requiring to be thus studied and thus taught, then, as a distinguished lawyer has remarked, 'a university will best consult its own dignity in declining to teach it.' This is the plow to which our ancestors here in America set their hand, and to which we have set ours; and we must see to it that the furrow is handsomely turned.

"But who is there, I may be asked, to study law in this way? Who is to have the time for it and the opportunity? Let me ask a question in return, and answer it. Who is it that studies the natural or physical sciences, engineering, philology, history, theology, or medical science in this way? First of all, those who, for any reason, propose to master these subjects, to make true

* "University Teaching of English Law." Address before the American Bar Association, Detroit, August 27, :895.

and exact statements of them, and to carry forward in these regions the limits of human knowledge, and especially the teachers of these things; second, not in so great a degree, but each as far as he may, the leaders in the practical application of these branches of knowledge to human affairs; third, in a still less degree, yet in some degree, all practitioners of these subjects, if I may use that phrase, who wish to understand their business and to do it thoroughly well.

"Precisely the same thing is true in law as in these or any other of the great parts of human knowledge. In all it is alike beneficial and alike necessary for the vigorous and fruitful development of the subject, for the best performance of the every-day work of the calling to which they relate, and for the best carrying out of the plain, practical duties of each man's place, that somewhere, and by some persons, these subjects should be investigated with the deepest research and the most searching critical study.

"The time has gone by when it was necessary to vindicate the utility of deep and lifelong investigations into the nature of electricity and the mode of its operation; into the nature of light, and heat, and sound, and the laws that govern their action; into the minute niceties of the chemical and physiological laboratory, the speculations and experiments of geology, or the absorbing calculations of the mathematician or astronomer. Men do not now need to be told what it is that has given them the steam-engine, the telegraph, the telephone, the electric railway and the electric light, the telescope, the improved lighthouse, the lucifer match, antiseptic surgery, the prophylactics against small-pox and diphtheria, aluminum the new metal, and the triumphs of modern engineering. These things are mainly the outcome of what seemed to the majority of mankind useless and unpractical study and experiment.

"But, as regards our law, those who press the importance of thorough and scientific study are not yet exempt from the duty of pointing out the use of it and its necessity. To say nothing of the widespread skepticism among a certain class of practical men, in and out of our profession, as to the advantages of everything of the sort, there is also, among those who nominally admit it, and even advocate it, a remarkable failure to appreciate what this admission means. It is the simple truth that you cannot have thorough and first-rate training in law any more than in physical science, unless you have a body of learned teachers; and you cannot have a learned faculty of law unless, like other faculties, they give their lives to the work. The main secret of teaching law, as of all teaching, is what Socrates declared to be the secret of eloquence—understanding your subject; and that requires, as regards any one of the great heads of our law, in the present stage of our science, an enormous and absorbing amount of labor."

This separation, which I have tried to describe, exists only in America. For this separation, the popular desire to reach these professions by short cuts, and the popular distrust of those who have done so, are equally responsible.

Our people have always been willing to tax themselves to furnish a general education for their children. The common-school idea from the very first has included a liberal education. But in most of the States the people have at one time or another definitely refused to devote public funds to the making of lawyers and doctors. They would not, at their expense, help men into professions they believed to be overpaid as well as overcrowded. This policy has been a most shortsighted one. It has been responsible for the existence in every part of our country of hordes of pettifoggers and quacks, who rob the people instead of serving them. Incompetent professional service is always robbery. The professions are overcrowded simply because they have ceased to be professions. The remedy for incompetence is found in insisting on competence. This can be done by furnishing means by which competence can be possible.

The forces which have operated here are necessarily associated with the growth of democracy. The movement of civilization has been constantly in the direction of the extension of the powers and privileges of the few to the many. By this influence careers and distinctions once reserved for the aristocracy have been opened to the common man. One immediate result — temporary, I believe, — is that the common man has invaded these provinces without abating one whit of his commonness. This is a necessary phase of the vulgarization which follows the extension of justice known as democracy. It is connected with the vulgarization of the press, the theater, the pulpit, which must follow their adjustment to the needs of the many, rather than to the finer tastes or juster judgment of the few. The common man is satisfied with common lawyers. When he ceases to be thus satisfied, he is no longer common. That his freedom of choice and the training which results from it will, in the long run, eliminate this vulgarization, is the justification for democracy. Our hope for the future lies largely in our recognition of the badness of the present. From the weakness of our professional schools the common man is the chief sufferer. And already he is joining in the demand that these schools be made better. It is one virtue of democracy that it is free to meet its own demands. It is absolutely certain that those schools whose work is most thorough and whose requirements are most exacting will have the most students, as well as the best ones. It is not true that the students of America demand poor instruction because it is cheap.

Notwithstanding all adverse conditions, there have been many great teachers of law in America, as there have been and are many great lawyers. The great teacher makes his influence felt, whatever the defects in the organization of the institution which claims his services. The present strength of the University of Michigan rests in large degree on the work of Thomas M. Cooley. The work of John B. Minor in the University of Virginia gave a well-deserved prominence to the Virginia School of Law. Theodore Dwight was once the Law School of Columbia College. Other law professors have added in no small degree to the prestige of Harvard, Cornell, and the University of Pennsylvania. In all these institutions a strenuous effort has been made to place the work in law on a basis not less high than that occupied by history and economics. In other words, in these and in some other institutions the law faculty is to be not an ''annex,'' but an integral part of the faculty of the university. When this is done, the requirements for graduation as a lawyer will not be less than equivalent to the work for which a degree would be granted to a chemist or a civil engineer.

To find the cause of any deficiency is to go a long way toward curing it.   In this case, it seems to me, the remedy lies in placing the instruction in law on the same footing as that of other departments of the university. The teaching of law should be a life work in itself.   The requirements and methods in law should be abreast of the best work in any department.   The university atmosphere and the university ideals should surround the student in law as well as the student in history.   No one should be encouraged to take professional studies until he is capable of carrying them on seriously and successfully.

There is, moreover, no reason for segregating the teachers of law in any way from the other members of the university faculty.   As well make chemistry or economics a separate school, as to set off the law by itself.   All these separations may be made in name, but they should not exist in fact.   The elements of law have as strong claim to a place in general education as the elements of geometry or psychology.   Even for purpose of professional education, it is better that the study of law should be carried on simultaneously with that of the historical and social sciences, which are its natural associates.   The basis of law is in the nature of man, not in the statutes of the United States, nor in those of England.   The common law has it source in man and his civilization, not in the books.   This the student must learn to know and feel.   So history, social science, and law must be mutually dependent on one another.   The student of the one cannot be ignorant of the others.

The suggestion that social studies should accompany
rather than precede law studies has lately received the
strong advocacy of Dr. Woodrow Wilson and Professor
Ernest W. Huffcut.* This association should give to
the student not only a lawyer's training, but a scholar's
horizon. Without this, broad views in jurisprudence
and in politics are impossible. Such a course of study
would give dignity to the general culture of the college.
A student takes a better hold on culture studies where
they are clearly related to the work of his life.

Moreover, the politicians of each country are for the
most part its lawyers. Our lawyers are our rulers.† We

* Professor Huffcut says: "We may safely give our assent to the plan
whereby the study of law is to be treated like the study of any other branch
of human knowledge; that the preparation for it should be mainly the same
as for the study of history and political science; and the law, upon the one
hand, and history, political science, and philosophy, upon the other, will
profit from the closer union between the two. I confess that this plan has for
me personally many attractive features. It drives out at the outset the professional or technical atmosphere which is likely to surround the law when
disconnected from other human interests. It brings the law school into the
warmth and color and light of a general university atmosphere. It relates
the subject of law logically and consistently to the general field of political
science. The student from the outset of his studies in the field of law is
encouraged, if not compelled, to make constant investigations in history, political science, and government, which cannot fail to give him a broader apprehension of the true meaning and import of legal institutions and the administration of justice. Our law schools are parts of a university system. By
making them organic parts of such system, asking our colleagues of the universities to recognize that our work is part and parcel of their own, and ourselves frankly recognizing that theirs is essential to the success of ours, we
shall yet arrive at a solution of our problem which shall advance the interests
of legal education and of sound learning." (Huffcut: Transactions American Bar Association, Detroit, 1895.)

† Mr. James DeWitt Andrews says: "One might almost say that this was
a government of the lawyers by the lawyers. Of the lawyers, because of the
prominent, almost controlling, part they played in its institutions; by the lawyers, because of the important part they have taken in its administration.
In every branch of government — legislative, executive, and judicial,— lawyers
have always predominated; but so well have they borne in mind the ethics of
the profession, that their office, whether in the administration of justice or

L

can never hope to see our State well governed till its lawyers are well trained. Our greatness has been in large degree the work of our great jurists. To know the law — not merely the statutes, or the tricks for evading them, — makes men great. Of these we have had many, though scant our provision for their training has been. There can be no political conscience except as an outcome of political knowledge. Right acting can only come as a result of right thinking. The men who think right will, in the long run, act in accord with their knowledge. Those who have known that there is a science of human institutions can never wholly forget that fact. There can be no right thinking in matters of public administration without a knowledge of the laws of growth of human institutions. Only in accordance with these laws is good government possible. Of these fundamental laws of being the statutes of man must be an expression. Where they are not so the people have sooner or later a fearful score to pay. The Fates charge compound interest on every human blunder, and they have their own way at the last.

when coupled with other public trusts, is but an agency and a trust, that their real supremacy has never been felt. Whoever impugns the integrity of the profession at large casts a slur on the nation." (Andrews: "The Works of James Wilson," Vol. I, preface.")

X.

THE PRACTICAL EDUCATION.

A PRACTICAL education is one which can be made effective in life. We often abuse the word *practical* by making it synonymous with temporary or superficial. It should mean just the opposite. An education which takes but little time and less effort, and leads at once to a paying situation, is not *practical*. It is not good, because it will never lead to anything better. An education which does not disclose the secret of power is unworthy the name. Nothing is really practical which does not provide for growth in effectiveness. There is nothing more practical than knowledge, nothing more unpractical than ignorance ; nothing more practical than sunshine, nothing less so than darkness. The chief essentials of education should be thoroughness and fitness. The most thorough training is the most practical, provided only that it is fitted to the end in view. The essential fault of educational systems of the past is that, in search for breadth and thoroughness, the element of fitness was forgotten. We have tried, as we used to say, to make well-rounded men, "men who stand four-square to every wind that blows." This is a training better fitted for hitching-posts or windmills than for men. This is the day of special knowledge. Only by doing some one thing better than any one else, can a man find a worthy place in our complex social fabric. The ability to do a hundred things in an inferior way will not help him. This is a fact our schools must recognize. No man is great by chance in these days. If one is to do anything of importance he must first understand what he is to do, and then set about it with all his might.

Men of affairs often sneer at college men and college methods. Some of their criticisms are justified, others not. Such justification as they may have had is found in the lack of fitness in college training. Among conditions of life infinitely varied the college has decreed that all boys should take the same studies, in the same way, and at the same time, and that these studies should be the routine of the English boy of a century ago. In thus repeating the thoughts and learning of nations half forgotten, the minds of some "Greek-minded" and "Roman-minded" men were stimulated to their highest activity, and for them such training was good and adequate.

But there were some, "American-minded" perhaps, whose powers were not awakened by such influences. These came forth from the college walls into the life of the world, as Rip Van Winkle from the Catskills, dazed by the new experiences to which their studies had given no clue.

I do not wish to depreciate the value of classical training. There is a higher point of view than that of mere utility, and the beautiful forms and noble thoughts of ancient literature have been a lifelong source of inspiration to thousands who have made no direct use of their college studies in the affairs of life. But there are other sources of inspiration which, in their way, may affect many to whom Latin or Greek would be a meaningless

grind. For such as these a different training is necessary, if our education is to be practical. The schools
of the future will avoid not only bad training, but also
"misfit" training; for the time of the student is so
precious that no part of it should be wrongly used.

The remedy for the evils of misfit training is not to
discard the high standards or the thorough drill of the
old college, but to apply it to a wider range of studies.
No two students are ever quite alike, and no two will
ever follow exactly the same career. If we work to the
best advantage, no two will ever follow the same course
of study. And thus recognizing in our efforts the
infinite variations of human nature, the work of higher
education acquires an effectiveness which it could never
have under the cast-iron systems of the traditional college. Misfit training is good only as compared with no
training at all. Any sort of activity is better than stag-
nation.

The purpose of right training is to prepare for work
which is to last. There is enough already of poor and
careless work. Whatever is done needs to be done
well. Let it be done honestly — not as to-day's make-
shift, but as done for all time.

High under the roof of the Cathedral of Cologne
there is many an image carved in stone and wrought
with the most exquisite care, but which human eye has
never seen since it was first placed in the niche in which
it stands. This work of the Gothic sculptors was done
for the sight of God, and not for the worship of man.
The Cathedral of Cologne was almost a thousand years
in building. I saw, the other day, a cathedral in one
of our Eastern cities, built in barely as many weeks as

the other in centuries. The marble sculptures on its lofty towers are made of sheet-iron, zinc-lined, and painted to represent stone. Such is the work of modern cathedral builders. But the slow-moving centuries will show the difference.

A Swiss watchmaker said the other day: "Your American manufacturers cannot establish themselves in Europe. The first sample you send is all right, the second lot begins to drop off, the third destroys your reputation, and the fourth puts an end to your trade. All you seem to care for is to make money. What you want is some pride in your work." If this has been true of American watchmakers, it should be true no longer. The work that lasts must be not the quickest, but the best. Let it be done, not to require each year a fresh coat of paint, but done as if to last forever, and some of it will endure. This world is crowded on its lower floor, but higher up, for centuries to come, there will still remain a niche for each piece of honest work.

"Profligacy," says Emerson, "consists not in spending, but in spending off the line of your career. The crime which bankrupts men and States is job work, declining from your main design to serve a turn here or there. Nothing is beneath you, if in the direction of your life; nothing, to you, is great or desirable, if it be off from that."

The test of civilization is the saving of labor. The great economic waste of the world is that involved in unskilled labor. The gain of the nineteenth century over the eighteenth is the gain of skill in workmanship. But with all our progress in labor-saving, we have yet far to go before our use of labor shall balance our waste of it. The work which goes to waste in Europe, even now, through lack of training and lack of proper tools, is greater than all the losses through wars and standing armies and the follies of hereditary caste. It is second only to the waste due to idleness itself. For idleness there is no remedy so effective as training. To know how to do is to have a pride and pleasure in doing. In the long run, there is no force making for virtue and sobriety so strong as the influence of skill.

If a man knows how to do and how to act, he is assured against half the dangers which beset life. Training of the hand, training of the mind, training of any kind, which gives the man the power to do something which he knows to be genuine, gives him self-respect, makes a man of him, not a tool, or a force, or a thing.

An unskilled laborer is a relic of past ages and conditions. He is a slave in a time when enforced slavery is past. The waste which comes from doing poor things in poor ways keeps half of humanity forever poor. What the unskilled man can do, a bucket of coal and a bucket of water, guided by "a thimbleful of brains," will do more effectively. It is the mission of industrial training to put an end to unskilled labor; to make each workman a free man. When the time shall come when each workman can use his powers to the best advantage we shall have an end to the labor problem. The final answer of the labor problem is that each should solve it for himself.

I have spoken of the training of the hand; but all training belongs to the brain, and all kinds of training are of like nature. The hand is the servant of the brain, and can receive nothing of itself. There is no such thing as manual training as distinguished from training of the intellect. There is brain behind every act of the hand. The muscles are the mind's only servants. Whether we speak of training an orator, a statesman, or a merchant, or a mechanic, the same language must be used. The essential is that the means should lead toward the end to be reached.

An ignorant man is a man who has fallen behind our civilization and cannot avail himself of his light. He finds himself in darkness, in an unknown land. He stumbles over trifling obstacles because he does not understand them. He cannot direct his course. The real dangers are all hidden, while the most innocent rock or bush seems a menacing giant. He is not master of the situation. We have but one life to live; let that be an effective one, not one that wastes at every turn through the loss of knowledge or lack of skill. What sunlight is to the eye education is to the intellect, and the most thorough education is always the most practical. No traveler is contented to go about with a lantern when he could as well have the sun. If he can have a compass and a map also, so much the better. But let his equipment be fitting. Let him not take an ax if there be no trees to chop, nor a boat unless he is to cross a river, nor a Latin grammar if he is to deal with bridge-building, unless the skill obtained by mastering the one gives him insight into the other.

I often meet parents who wish to give their sons a practical education. They think of practical as something cheap and easy. A little drawing, a little tinkering with machinery, a little bookkeeping of imaginary accounts, and their sons are "ready for business." "Ready for business,'' as though the complex problems of finance were to be solved by a knowledge of bookkeeping by double-entry! Life is more serious than that. It takes a thorough education to make a successful business man. Not the education of the schools, we say,—and it may be so; but if so, it is the fault of the schools. They ought to make good business men as well as to make good men in any other profession. They ought to fit men for life. Why do the great majority of merchants fail? Is it not because they do not know how to succeed? Is it not because they have not the brains and the skill to compete with those who had both brains and training? Is it not because they do not realize that there are laws of finance and commerce as inexorable as the law of gravitation? A man will stand erect because he stands in accord with the law of gravitation. A man or a nation will grow rich by working in accord with the laws which govern the accumulation of wealth. If there are such laws, men should know them. What men must know the schools can teach.

The schools will indeed do a great work if they teach the existence of law. Half the people of America believe this is a world of chance. Half of them believe they are victims of bad luck when they receive the rewards of their own stupidity. Half of them believe that they are favorites of fortune, and will be helped out somehow, regardless of what they may do. Now and then some man catches a falling apple, picks up a penny from the dust, or a nugget from the gulch. Then his neighbors set to looking into the sky for apples, or into the dust for pennies, as though pennies and apples come in that way. Waiting for chances never made anybody

rich.   The Golden Age of California began when gold
no longer came by chance.   There is more gold in the
black adobe of the Santa Clara Valley than existed in
the whole great range of the Sierras until men sought
for it, not by luck or chance, but by system and science.
Whatever is worth having comes because we have earned
it.   There is but one way to earn anything — that is to
find out the laws which govern production, and to shape
our actions in accordance with these laws.   Good luck
never comes to the capable man as a surprise.   He is
prepared for it, because it was the very thing he has
a right to expect.   Sooner or later, and after many hard
raps, every man who lives long enough will find this
out.   When he does so, he has the key to success,
though it may be too late to use it.

It is the work of the school to give these laws reality
in the mind of the student.   The school can bring the
student face to face with these laws, and even teach him
to make them do his bidding.   If we work with them,
these laws are as tractable as the placid flow of a mighty
river.   If we struggle against them, they make the terrible havoc of an uncontrolled flood.   To ignore them
is to defy them.   From our knowledge of the laws of nature arise the achievements of civilization.   These are our
knowledge wrought into action.   The thing we understand becomes our servant.   Whatever we know we can
have.   But whatever we conquer, our victory is a tri-
umph of knowledge.

We speak of this age as the age of inventions, the age
of man's conquest of the forces of nature.   But the man
who invents or constructs machinery is not the conqueror.
It is easy for one to harness the lightning when another

has shown him the lightning's nature and ways. It is easier still to repeat what others have done. The applications of science are only an incident in the growth of science. The electric light and the locomotive follow sooner or later, as a matter of course, when we have found the laws which govern electric currents and the expansive power of steam. It is this knowledge which gives control over the forces of nature. It is by investigation, not through application or repetition, that man's power advances. It is the investigator who comes in contact with the unveiled ways of God. The applications of electricity to common purposes have been for the most part made in our day, but the knowledge on which they are based goes back to the earliest investigators of physical laws. These men forced their way into the infinite darkness, regardless of the multitude that would crowd into their path. An investigator is the cause of a thousand inventors. A Faraday or a Helmholtz is the parent of a thousand Edisons. Without the help of the university Edisons are possible. Only the highest training can make a Helmholtz; for no man can reach the highest rank who has not entered into all the work of all his predecessors.

And this brings me to say that the great work of a university is to be the center of investigation. It should be the source of new truths — of new conquests in every field. To it will come for the brief course of training and guidance many who, in the maturity of their lives, will accomplish much good for their fellow-men. In the ever-increasing circle of human knowledge new fields are being constantly opened. The whole knowledge of the last generation must be taken for granted as the basis of

advancement for the next.   Not till the circle of human
knowledge has widened to infinity, shall we comprehend
the infinite goodness of God.

XI.

SCIENCE IN THE HIGH SCHOOL.*

THE purpose of science-teaching as a part of general education is this — to train the judgment through its exercise on first-hand knowledge. The student of science is taught to know what he knows and to distinguish it from what he merely remembers or imagines. Our contact with the universe is the source of all our knowledge. This knowledge tested and set in order we call science. Throughout the ages, the growth of the human mind has been in direct proportion to the breadth of this contact. To the man without knowledge of science, the universe seems small. Science is our perception of realities; and as the realities come, year by year, to occupy a larger and larger place in our life, so the demand for more and better training in science will long be an urgent and growing one. But science should hold its place in the schools by virtue of its power as an agent in mental training, not because of the special usefulness of scientific facts, nor because knowledge of things has a higher market value than the knowledge of words.

The time will come when the study of the objects and forces of nature will be as much a matter of course in all our schools as the study of numbers, but the science-work of the next century will not be the work we are

*Address before the Indiana State Teachers' Association, December 26, 1889 ; published in the Popular Science Monthly, April, 1890.

doing now. The science in our schools is too often a make-believe, and the schools gain with every make-believe that slips out of the curriculum. Deeply as I am interested in the progress of science, both in school and out, with Professor Huxley, "I would not turn my hand over" to have biology taught in every school in the land, if the subject be taught through books only. To pretend to do, without doing, is worse than not to pretend. The conventional "fourteen weeks" in science gives no contact with nature, no training of any sort, no information worth having; only a distaste for that class of scattering information which is supposed to be science.

There is a charm in real knowledge which every student feels. The magnet attracts iron, to be sure, to the student who has learned the fact from a book; but the fact is real only to the student who has himself felt it pull. It is more than this — it is enchanting to the student who has discovered the fact for himself. To read a statement of the fact gives knowledge, more or less complete, as the book is accurate or the memory retentive. To verify the fact gives training; to discover it gives inspiration. Training and inspiration, not the facts themselves, are the justification of science-teaching. Facts enough we can gather later in life, when we are too old to be trained or inspired. He whose knowledge comes from authority, or is derived from books alone, has no notion of the force of an idea brought first-hand from human experience.

What is true of one science is true of all in greater or less degree. I may take the science of zoology for my illustration, simply because it is the one nearest my hand. In very few of our high schools has the instruction in zoology any value. For this unfortunate fact there are several causes, and some of these are beyond the control of the teachers. In the first place, the high-school course is overloaded, and the small part of the course given to the sciences is divided among too many of them. A smattering of one science is of little use, either for discipline or information. A smattering of many sciences may be even worse, because it leads the mind to be content with smattering. Indeed, so greatly have our schools sinned in this respect that many writers on education seem to regard science as synonymous with smattering, and they contrast it with other branches of learning which are supposed to have some standard of thoroughness. Most of our colleges have, at one time or other, arranged courses of study not approved by the faculty, in response to the popular demand for many studies in a little time. Such a course of odds and ends is always called "the scientific course," and it leads to the appropriate degree of "B. S.,"—Bachelor of Surfaces.

The high school can do some things very well, but it will fail if it try to do too much. Unfortunately, the present tendency in our high schools is in the direction of such failure — to do many things poorly, rather than a few things well. In other words, we try to satisfy the public by a show of teaching those subjects which we do not really teach. In the sciences we study books instead of nature, because books are plenty and cheap, and can be finished quickly, while Nature herself is accessible only to those who want something of her. The high school would do well not to attempt to give a general view of science. It is better to select some two or three

of the number — a physical and a biological science, perhaps,— and to spend the available time on these.   The
choice should depend mainly on the interest or the skill
of the teacher.   Teach those sciences that you can teach
best.

President Hill, of Rochester, has well said: "Thousands of our youth have studied chemistry without ever
seeing an experiment, physics without seeing an air-pump,
and astronomy without ever looking through a telescope.
A professor of the ancient type maintained that this is a
great advantage, like the study of geometry without
figures, because it stimulates the imagination.   It is an
invigoration of stupidity and conceit, sealing the mind to
reality by substituting subjective fancies for experimental
proofs, and the pretense of knowing for clear ideas.   Its
effect upon the morals is as pernicious as its effect upon
the mind; for it weakens the reverence for truth and
engenders the habit of mental trifling."

One of our wisest writers on education excludes science-teaching (by which he means giving information
about scientific subjects) from the fundamental requirements of education, because the knowledge of nature is
not one of the "five windows" through which the soul
looks .out on life.   These windows, according to this
author, are reading and writing, grammar, arithmetic,
geography, and history.   The simile is a happy one.
The soul, confined in the watch-tower of medieval education, looks out on the world through these five windows
— and they are but windows, for they give no contact
with the things themselves.   The study of nature throws
wide open the doors, and lets the soul out to the fields
and woods.   It brings that contact with God through

His works which has been, tnrough all the ages, the inspiration of the poets and the prophets, as well as of those long-despised apostles of truth whom we call men of science.

A second difficulty is this: Our towns will not pay for teachers enough to do the work as it should be done, and of the few teachers we have the people make no demand for thorough preparation. Very few of them are broadly educated or have had any scientific training whatever. And such teachers are expected to teach a dozen subjects each, and therefore have no time to make good their defective preparation. Thus good teaching of science cannot be expected, for streams do not rise higher than their sources. The only remedy for these conditions seems to lie in the gradual education of the people. A series of object-lessons, showing the difference between a good teacher and a poor one, is the most effective means of causing good work to be appreciated.

But, taking things as they are, even with uneducated teachers and teachers crowded for time, fairly good work may be done by the use of good methods. A great deal will depend, not on the kind of books you use, but on the kind of books you avoid. Most of the current textbooks of elementary zoology are simply pernicious so far as your purposes are concerned. Even if these books were well digested and accurate in their statements of fact, which is rarely the case, they are based on incorrect principles. They are not elementary but fragmentary in their character. It is a great mistake to suppose that because a book is small and says very little about each one of the animals of which it treats, it is thereby rendered elementary. Fragments are not necessarily elements. A frag-

M

ment of rock is as hard to digest as a bowlder.   Elementary work in science should treat of but few things, but the impressions it leaves with the child should be very clear ones.   The ideas derived from the common text-books are of the vaguest possible character.   These books are the parasites, not the allies, of science.   They bear the same relation to the progress of science that barnacles bear to the progress of a ship.   If you keep clear of these, you cannot go far astray.   Let us recall the words of Agassiz to the publisher who tried to induce him to write a school-book on zoology:

"I told him," he said, "that I was not the man to do that sort of thing; and I told him, too, that the less of that sort of thing which is done the better.   It is not school-books we want, but students.   The book of nature is always open, and all I can do or say shall be to lead students to study that book, and not to pin their faith to any other."   And at another time he said, "If we study Nature in books, when we go out of doors we cannot find her."

The essential of method is that we allow nothing to come between the student and the object which he studies.   The book, or chart, or lecture which can be used in place of the real thing is the thing you should never use.   Your students should see for themselves, and draw their own conclusions from what they see.   When they have a groundwork of their own observations, other facts can be made known to them as a basis for advanced generalizations, for the right use of books is as important as their misuse is pernicious; but work of this sort belongs to the university rather than to the high school. You do not wish to have your students tell you from memory the characters of the *Sauropsida* as distinguished from the *Ichthyopsida*. What you want is the answer to their own questionings of the frog and the turtle.

I was lately present at a high-school examination in zoology. The teacher gave a number of the stock questions, such as "Describe the Gasteropoda," "What are the chief differences between the domestic turkey and the turkey of Honduras?" "How do Asiatic and African elephants differ?" "On which foot of the ornithorhynchus does the webbing extend past the toes?" and so on. At last he said: "I will now give you a practical question: A few days ago we had a frog in the class, and all of you saw it; now write out all the characteristics of the sub-kingdom, class, and order to which the frog belongs."

This is all useless. The definitions of these classes and orders do not concern the child. To the working naturalist, these names are as essential as the names of the stations on the road to a railway engineer. They belong to his business, but the names and distances of railway stations do not form part of any good work in primary geography. You do not need to teach your students that vertebrates are divided into mammals, birds, reptiles, batrachians, and fishes. It is not true in the first place, and, if it were, it is not relevant to them. Stick to your frog, if you are studying frogs, and he will teach you more of the science of animals than can be learned from all the memorized classifications that you can bracket out on a hundred rods of blackboard!

The prime defect in our schools is not, after all, that the teachers do not know the subjects they teach, but that they do not know nor care for the purpose of their teaching. In other words, they do not know how to teach. The book is placed in their hands by the school board, and they teach by the book. If the book comes to them wrong-side up, their teaching is forever inverted. That this is true, the statistics gathered recently from the high schools of Indiana, by Dr. Barton W. Evermann, very clearly show. It is no wonder that a superintendent is needed for every dozen teachers. A good teacher should know the end for which he works, and then he can adapt his means to fit this end.

I once visited a large high school, one of the best in the country, with a science-teacher whose studies have won him the respect of his fellow-workers. But for some reason, on that day at least, he failed to bring himself into the classroom. I heard him quizzing a class of boys and girls on animals — not on the animals of the woods and fields, not on the animals before them, for there were none, but on the edentates of South America. An especial point was to find out whether it is the nine-banded armadillo *(novemcinctus)* or the three-banded armadillo *(tricinctus)* which does not dig a hole in the ground for its nest. The book, written by a man who did not know an armadillo from a mud-turtle, gives this piece of information. It was in the lesson, and the students must get it. And on this and like subjects these boys and girls were wasting their precious time — precious, because if they do not learn to observe in their youth, they will never learn, and the horizon of their lives will be always narrower and darker than it should have been. Already the work of that day is a blank. They have forgotten the nine-banded armadillo and the three-banded, and so has their teacher, and so have I. All that remains with them is a mild hatred of the armadillo and of the edentates in general, and a feeling of relief at being no longer under their baleful influence. But with this usually goes the determination never to study zoology again. And when these students later come to the college, they know no more of science and its methods than they did when in babyhood they first cried for the moon.

Darwin tells us that his early instruction in geology was so "incredibly dull" that he came to the determination, afterward happily changed, "never so long as he lived to read a book on geology or in any way to study the subject."

I once had a student, well trained in the conventional methods of non-science, who was set to observe the yeast-plant under the microscope. He had read what the books say about yeast, and had looked at the pictures. So he went to work vigorously. In a short time he had found out all about the little plant, and had made a series of drawings which showed it very nicely. By and by some one noticed that he was working without any object-glass in his microscope. He had not seen the yeast-plant at all, only the dust on the eye-piece. This is the vital fault of much of our teaching of elementary science. It is not real; it is not the study of nature, only of the dust-heaps of old definitions.

Yet nothing is easier than to do fairly good teaching, even without special knowledge or special appliances. Bring out your specimens and set them before the boys and girls. They will do the work, and do it eagerly; and they will furnish the specimens, too. There is no difficulty about materials. Our New World is the " El

Dorado" of the naturalists of Europe. You can get material for a week's work by turning over a single rotten log. I once heard Professor Agassiz say to an assembly of teachers, and I quote from him the more freely because he gave his life to the task of the introduction of right methods into American schools:

"Select such subjects that your students can not walk out without seeing them. If you can find nothing better, take a house-fly or a cricket, and let each one hold a specimen while you speak. . . . There is no part of the country where, in the summer, you cannot get a sufficient supply of the best of specimens. Teach your pupils to bring them in. Take your text from the brooks and not from the booksellers. . . . It is better to have a few forms well studied than to teach a little about many hundred species. Better a dozen forms thoroughly known as the result of the first year's work, than to have two thousand dollars' worth of shells and corals bought from a curiosity-store. The dozen animals will be your own. . . . You will find the same elements of instruction all about you wherever you are teaching. You can take your classes out and give them the same lessons, and lead them up to the same subjects in one place as another. And this method of teaching children is so natural, so suggestive, so true. That is the charm of teaching from Nature. No one can warp her to suit his own views. She brings us back to absolute truth so often as we wander."

XII.

SCIENCE AND THE COLLEGES.*

WE have come together to-day to do our part in raising one of the milestones which mark the progress of education in America. Our interest in higher education and our interest in science bring us here. More than ever before in the history of humanity we find these interests closely associated. More and more each year the higher education of America is taking the character of science ; and in the extension of human knowledge, the American university now finds its best excuse for being.

I hope that in what I shall have to say I shall not be accused of undue glorification of science. I recognize in the fullest degree the value of all agencies in the development of the human mind. But the other departments of learning may each have its turn. We are here to-day to dedicate a hall of science. We are here in the interest of science-teaching and scientific research. When, in a few years to come, we may dedicate a hall of letters, we shall sing the praises of poetry and literature. But to-day we speak of science, in the full certainty that the humanities will not suffer with its growth. All real knowledge is a help to all other, and all real love of beauty must rest on love of truth.

At this time, as we stand together, by the side of the

* Address at the dedication of the Science Hall of the University of Illinois, November 16, 1892; from the Popular Science Monthly for April, 1893.

milestone we have set up, on the breezy upland which marks the boundary of our nineteenth century, it is worth while for a moment to glance back over the depressing lowlands from which we have risen. And in our discussion of the relations of the American college to science, we find depression and darkness enough without going back very far.

I am still numbered, I trust, with the young men. I am sure that I have never yet heard the word "old" seriously joined to my name. When men speak of "Old Jordan," I know that they mean the river of Palestine, and not me. Yet, in the few years during which I have taught zoology, the relation of science to education has undergone most remarkable changes.

I remember very clearly that twenty years ago, when, in such way as I could, I had prepared myself for the two professions of naturalist and college professor, I found that these professions were in no way related. I remember having in 1872 put the results of my observations into these words : " The colleges have no part or interest in the progress of science, and science has no interest in the growth of the colleges."

The college course in those days led into no free air. *A priori* and *ex cathedra*, two of its favorite phrases, described it exactly. Its essentials were the grammar of dead languages, and the memorized results of the applications of logic to number and space. Grammar and logic were taught in a perfunctory way, and the student exhausted every device known to restless boys in his desire to evade the instruction he had spent his time and money to obtain. Then, when all the drill was over, and the long struggle between perfunctory teachers and

unwilling boys had dragged to an end, the students were
passed on to the president, to receive from him an exposition of philosophy.   This was the outlook on life for
which three years of drill made preparation.   And this
philosophy was never the outgrowth of the knowledge
of the day, but simply the *débris* of outworn speculations
of the middle ages.   It bore no relations to modern life or
modern thought.   It was therefore peculiarly safe and
tranquilizing.

Let us recall the first invasion of science in the conventional programmes of study.   It came in response to an
outside demand for subjects interesting and practical.   It
was met in such a way as to silence, rather than to satisfy, the demand.   A few trifling courses, memorized
from antiquated text-books, and the work in science was
finished.   The teachers who were capable of higher
things had no opportunity to make use of their powers.
Their investigations were not part of their duties.   They
were carried on in time stolen from their tasks of plod-
ding and prodding.   It is to the shame of the State of
Indiana that she kept one of the greatest astronomers
of our time for forty years teaching boys the elements of
geometry and algebra.   That he should have taught
astronomy, and made astronomers, occurred to no one
in authority until Daniel Kirkwood was seventy years
old, and by the laws of nature could teach no longer.
What was true in this case was true in scores of others.
The investigator had no part in the college system, or if
on sufferance he found a place, his time was devoted to
anything else rather than to the promotion of science.
Everywhere in Europe and America were men who were
devoting their lives eagerly to scientific research; but, in

nine cases out of ten, these men were outside of the colleges.   Even with the others, very few had any opportunity to teach those subjects in which the interest was deepest.

The American college of the middle of this century, like its English original, existed for the work of the church.   "If the college dies the church dies," was the basis of its appeal for money and influence.   Its duty was to form a class of educated men in whose hands should lie the preservation of the creed.   In the mouths of ignorant men the truths of the church would be clouded. Each wise church would see that its wisdom be not marred by human folly.   The needs of one church indicated the needs of others.   So it came about that each of the many organizations called churches in America established its colleges here and there about the country, all based on the same general plan.

And, as the little towns on the rivers and prairies grew with the progress of the country into large cities, so it was thought, by some mysterious virtue of inward expansion, these little schools in time would grow to be great universities.   And in this optimistic spirit the future was forestalled, and the schools were called universities from the beginning.   As time went on, it appeared that a university could not be made without money, and the source of money must be outside the schools.   And so has ensued a long struggle between the American college and the wolf at the door — a tedious, belittling conflict, which has done much to lower the name and dignity of higher education.   To this educational planting without watering, repeated again and again, East and West, North and South, must be ascribed the unnaturally severe struggle for existence through which our colleges have been forced to pass, the poor work, low salaries, and humiliating economies of the American college professor, the natural end of whom, according to Dr. Holmes, is "starvation."

The intense rivalry among these schools, like rivalry among half-starving tradesmen, has done much to belittle the cause in which all are engaged. At the same time, their combined rivalry has too often prevented the growth within their neighborhood of any better school.

In this connection, you may pardon me for a word of my own experience, when twenty years ago (1872) I set out in search of a place for work. A chair of natural history was the height of my aspirations; for anything more specialized than this it seemed useless to hope. I was early called from New York to such a chair, in a well-known college of Illinois. But in those days, the work attached to a college chair was never limited by its title. As professor of natural history, I taught zoology, botany, geology, physiology — a little of each, and to little purpose. Then physics, chemistry, mineralogy, natural theology, and political economy, also, as a matter of course. With these went German, Spanish, and evidences of Christianity, because there was no one else to take them. There finally fell on me the literary work of the college — the orations, essays, declamations, and all that flavorless foolishness on which the college depended for a creditable display at commencement. When to this was added a class in the Sunday-school, you will see why it seemed necessary that the naturalist and the professor must sooner or later part company. I tried at one time to establish a little laboratory in chemistry, but met with a

sharp rebuke from the board of trustees, who directed
me to keep the students out of what was called the "cab-
inet," for they were likely to injure the apparatus and
waste the chemicals.

When I left this college and looked elsewhere for work,
I found on all sides difficulty and disappointment; for the
reputation I had, wholly undeserved, I am sorry to say,
was the dreaded reputation of a specialist.

The question of conventional orthodoxy seemed everywhere to be made one of primary importance, and candidates for chairs who, like myself, were not heretics on
the subject of the origin of species, passed the rock of
evolution, only to be stranded on the inner shoals of the
mysteries of the Scottish philosophy.

But these were not the only sources of difficulty. In
one institution toward which I had looked, the chair of
natural history was found unnecessary. In the meeting
of the board of trustees, a member arose and said, in substance: "We have just elected a professor of history.
This includes all history, and the work in natural history
is a part of it. Let the professor in history take this,
too." And for that year, at least, the professor of history took it all, and it was not hard for him to do this,
because the work in history was the cutting of straw.
He read a chapter in a text-book in advance of the students. This was no heavy drain on either his time or his
intellect. Even in the excellent State university into
which I ultimately drifted, I was met at the beginning by
the caution that the purpose of my work must be elementary teaching, the statement of the essential facts of
science, and by no means the making of naturalists or
of specialists.

I could give more illustrations, and from better institutions, showing that the demand of the colleges of twenty years ago was a demand for docility and versatility, rather than for thoroughness or originality; that, as a rule, the progress of science in America came from men outside of the college, and in a great part outside of college training and college sympathies; that to promote science or to extend knowledge was not often one of the college ideals; and that the college's chief function was to keep old ideas unchanged. What was safe in times of old will be safe to-day, and safety, rather than inspiration or investigation, was the purpose of the college. From time immemorial until now, Oxford and Cambridge, the schools of clergymen and gentlemen, have been the center of English conservatism. The American colleges — dilute copies of Oxford and Cambridge — came nearest their models in their retention of old methods and old ideas. The motto, once suggested for a scientific museum, "We will keep what we have got," might have been taken by the American college. There was no American university then, unless a few broad-minded teachers — mostly in Harvard, Yale, Princeton, and Michigan — could, as so many individuals, be properly regarded as such.

The coming of Agassiz to America may be said to mark the foundation of the first American university. Agassiz was the university. The essential character of the university is *Lernfreiheit*, freedom of learning, the freedom of the student to pursue his studies to the limit of the known, the freedom of encouragement to invade the realm of the unknown. It is from this realm that come the chief rewards of the scholar. The school from which no exploring parties set out has no right to the name of university.   In the progress of science, and the application of its methods to subjects not formerly considered scientific, the German university has its growth and development.   In like progress must arise the American university.

You remember the story of the discussion, some forty years ago, between Emerson and Agassiz, as to the future of Harvard.   Emerson, himself one of the sanest and broadest of men, saw in the work of Agassiz elements of danger, whereby the time-honored symmetry of Harvard might be destroyed.   In a lecture on universities, in Boston, Emerson made some such statement as this: That natural history was " getting too great an ascendency at Harvard"; that it " was out of proportion to other departments, 'and hinted' that a check-rein would not be amiss on the enthusiastic young professor who is responsible for this."

" Do you not see," Agassiz wrote to Emerson, "that the way to bring about a well-proportioned development of all the resources of the university is not to check the natural history department, but to stimulate all the others?   Not that the zoological school grows too fast, but that the others do not grow fast enough?   This sounds invidious and perhaps somewhat boastful; but it is you," he said, " and not I, who have instituted the comparison.   It strikes me that you have not hit upon the best remedy for this want of balance.   If symmetry is to be obtained by cutting down the most vigorous growth, it seems to me it would be better to have a little irregularity here and there.   In stimulating, by every means in my power, the growth of the museum and the means of education connected with it, I am far from having a selfish wish to see my own department tower above the others. I wish that every one of my colleagues would make it hard for me to keep up with him; and there are some among them, I am happy to say, who are ready to run a race with me."

In these words of Agassiz may be seen the key-note of modern university progress. The university should be the great refuge-hut on the ultimate boundaries of knowledge, from which, daily and weekly, adventurous bands set out on voyages of discovery. It should be the Upernavik from which Polar travelers draw their supplies, and as the shoreless sea of the unknown meets us on every side, the same house of refuge and supply will serve for a thousand different exploring parties, moving out in every direction into the infinite ocean. This is the university ideal of the future. Some day it will be felt as a loss and a crime if any one who could be an explorer is forced to become anything else. And even then, after countless ages of education and scientific progress, the true university will still stand on the boundaries, it walls still washed by the same unending sea, the boundless ocean of possible human knowledge.

The new growth of the American university which we honor to-day is simply its extension and its freedom, so that a scholar can find place within its walls. The scholar cannot breathe in confined air. The walls of medievalism have been taken down. The winds of freedom are blowing, and the summer sunshine of to-day quickens the pulse of the scholar in the deepest cloister. In the university of the future, all departments of human knowledge, all laws of the omnipresent God will be equally cherished because equally sacred.   The place of science in education will then be the place it deserves — nothing more, nothing less.

Many influences have combined to bring about the emancipation of the American college.   Not the least of these is the growth of the State university as an institution, existing for all the people, and for no end except the purpose of popular instruction.   It is a part of the great training-school in civics, morals, and economics which we call universal suffrage.

Most of these schools have celebrated their coming of age within the last five years, and their growth is certainly one of the most notable features in the intellectual development of America.   The State university was founded as a logical result of the American system of education.   It was part of the graded system through which the student was to rise, step by step, from the township school to the State university.   It has grown because it deserved to grow.   When it has deserved nothing, it has received nothing.   In the persistence of old methods and low ideals we find the reason for the slow growth of some of the State universities.   In the early dropping of shackles and the loyalty to its own freedom we find the cause of the rapid growth of others.

In its early years the State university was in aim and method almost a duplicate of the denominational schools by which it was surrounded.   Its traditions were the same, its professors drawn from the same source; its presidents were often the defeated candidates for presidencies of the denominational schools.   Men not popular enough for church preferment would do for the headship of the State universities. The salaries paid were very small, the patronage was local, and the professors were often chosen at the dictates of some local leader, or to meet some real or supposed local demand. I can remember one case when the country was searched to find for a State university a professor of history who should be a Democrat and a Methodist. All questions of fitness were subordinated to this one of restoring the lost symmetry of a school in which Presbyterians, Baptists, and Republicans had more than their share of the spoils. This idea of division of spoils in schools, as in politics, is only a shade less baleful than the still older one of taking all spoils without division. And when the spoils system was finally ignored, and in the State universities men were chosen with reference to their character, scholarship, and ability to teach, regardless of "other marks or brands" upon them, the position of professor was made dignified and worthy.

The first important step in the advance of the State universities came through the growth of individualism in education — that is, through the advent of the elective system,— and its first phase was the permission to substitute advanced work in science for elementary work in something else. It does not matter from what source the idea of individual choice in education has arisen. It may be a gift from far-seeing Harvard to her younger sisters; or it may be that in Harvard, as elsewhere, the elective system has arisen from a study of the actual conditions. The educational ideas which are now held by the majority of teachers in our larger schools were long ago the views of the overruled minority; and for fifty years or more individuals in the minority have looked forward to the time when inspiration, and not drill, would be the aim of the colleges.

Agassiz said, in 1864, in advocating the elective system, that although it might possibly give the pretext for easy evasion of duty to some inefficient or lazy students, it gave larger opportunities to the better class, and the university should adapt itself to the latter, rather than to the former. "The bright students," he said, "are now deprived of the best advantages to be had, because the dull or the indifferent must be treated like children."

In the same year, Emerson spoke of the old grudge he had for forty-five years owed Harvard College, for the cruel waste of two years of college time on mathematics, without any attempt to adapt the tasks to the capacity of learners. "I still remember," he said, "the useless pains I took, and my serious recourse to my tutor for aid he did not know how to give me. And now I see to-day the same indiscriminate imposing of mathematics on all students during two years. Ear, or no ear, you shall all learn music, to the waste of the time and health of a large part of the class."

I remember well the beginning of the modern system in the university of a neighboring State. It came as the permission, carefully guarded, to certain students, who had creditably passed the examination of the Freshman year in Latin, to take, instead of the Sophomore Latin, some advanced work in zoology. To the very great surprise of the professor of Latin, those who availed themselves of this opportunity "to take something easy" were not the worst students in Latin, but the best. Those who were attracted by investigation chose the new road; the plodders and shirks were contented with the evils they had, rather than to fly to others that they knew not of. And so, little by little, in that institution, and in all the others, has come about a relaxation of the chains of the curriculum of Oxford and Cambridge, and the extension of opportunities for students to find out the facts of nature for themselves, rather than to rest with the conserved wisdom of an incurious past.

Thus slowly and painfully came about the development of the scientific courses. We can all remember the dreary time when in the tedious faculty meetings we used to devise scientific courses, short in time and weak in quality, for students who could not, or would not, learn Latin and Greek. There was no scientific preparation or achievement required in these courses. They were scientific only in the sense that they were not anything else. Their degree of Bachelor of Science was regarded, and rightly, as far inferior to the time-honored B. A. In the inner circle of education it was regarded as no degree at all, and its existence was a concession to the utilitarian spirit of a non-scholastic age. The scientific course was, indeed, inferior; for it lacked substance. There was no lime in its vertebræ. The central axis of Greek had been taken out, and no corresponding piece of solid work put in its place. Gradually, however, even this despised degree has risen to a place with the others. Slowly and grudgingly the colleges have admitted that under some circumstances the study of science might be as worthy of recognition as the study of Greek. When science was worthily studied, this proposition became easy of acceptance. In our best colleges to-day the study of science stands side by side with the study of language, and the one counts equally with the other, even for the

degree of Bachelor of Arts.   For not the Greek itself,
but the culture it implies, was the glory of the course of
arts.   When equal culture and equal work come through
other channels, they are worthy of this degree.   To deny
this, would be to make of the degree itself a mere child's
toy, a play on words.   As a matter of fact, it can be
little more, and sooner or later the college will have no
need for degrees.   Science has shown herself a worthy
suitor of the highest degree the university can give.   She
will show herself strong enough to care for no degrees at
all.   In the great schools of the future, each study shall
become its own reward.   Let all come who will, and let
each take what he can, and let the ideals be so high that
no one will imagine that he is getting when he is not.

Not the least of the aids to freedom in science was the
Morrill Act, under which a certain part of the public
lands was given for the foundation of schools of applied
science.   Unhappily, much of this fund was wasted outright by thriftless management.   Much more was in some
States half-wasted by the formation of separate schools for
applied science, where State colleges of the old type already
existed.   Indeed, in many States, the college and the
technical school were so far separated, that the legislators
of 1868 saw in them nothing in common.   Nevertheless,
the highest wisdom in education is to bring the various
influences together wherever it is possible.   There is no
knowledge which is not science, and there can be no
applied science without the basis of pure science on which
to rest.   Schools of applied knowledge cannot be legiti-
mately separated from schools of knowledge.   But
whatever the use made of the money, the passage of the
Morrill Act in the interest of applied science has given

scientific work a prominence in our colleges it did not have before. It has given science definite rights in the curriculum where before it seemed to exist by sufferance.

I congratulate the State of Illinois that its university is one university; that its pure and applied science, its literature, history, philosophy, and art are taught in one institution, by one united faculty. The best results in any line of education cannot be reached without the association of all others. The training of the engineer will be the more valuable from his association with the classical student. The literary man may gain much, and will lose nothing, from his acquaintance with the practical work of the engineer. The separation of the schools founded by the Morrill Act from the State university, as we have seen in nearly half the States of the Union, was a blunder which time will deepen into a crime. With the union of the two has come the rapid growth of the universities of Wisconsin, California, Illinois, Minnesota, and Nebraska, when the higher work of the State is all concentrated in one place.

The freedom of choice has not worked to the advantage of science alone. The element of consent in college study has brought about a revival in classical education as well as in science. It is not certain even that more science studies are chosen by students, under the elective system than were taken on the old plan of a required curriculum. But the work is done in a different spirit. The colleges and the investigators are being drawn together. There is no line of investigation in which the college cannot help, if the investigators have freedom to use it. The scientific men are being drawn into sympathy with higher education. Men are now in college who under

the former system would have been self-made men, with
all the disadvantages that isolation implies.   Education
gives the ability to enter into the labors of others; and
the scientific man of to-day must use every advantage, if
he is to make his own work an advance in knowledge.
He must know what has been done by those who have
gone before him.   He must use their highest achievements as a basis for further progress.   Science cannot let
go of its past.   And to the self-made man of science,
struggle as he may, the books of the past are at least
partially closed.

Twenty-five years ago the college repelled rather
than aided men of science.   After a brief experience
in college, many men of scientific interests went away
and carried on their own studies in their own fashion.
And others similarly situated, with aspirations in literature, history, or engineering, stayed away, and grew
up untouched by the higher education of their times.
The elective system provides for such as these.   It not
only gives a new impulse to the students' work, but it
brings a new body of students under collegiate influences.

Nothing in our educational history has been more
remarkable than the increase in numbers of students in
our principal colleges, and the corresponding increase in
influence of these schools, within the last ten years.   Yet
nothing is more evident than the fact that these students
are not going to college in the old-fashioned sense.   The
old-fashioned college ideals are not rising in value; but
new possibilities of training and the inspiration of modern thought bring to the university all sorts and conditions of men and women whose predecessors twenty
years ago would not have thought of entering an Ameri-

can college. Where old educational ideas still reign, be the college rich or poor, there is no increase in numbers nor in influence. Unless a college education involves the emancipation of thought, unless it gives something to think about, it has no place in the educational system of the future. The future of our country will rest with college men, because the college of the future will meet the needs of all men of power, and draw them to its walls.

Scientific men have no wish to underestimate literary or classical training. The revolution in our higher education is not a revolt against the classics. It is an appeal from the assumption that the classics furnish the only gate to culture. It asserts the existence of a thousand gates — as many ways to culture as there are types of men. Scientific training asks only for freedom of development, and for the right to be judged by its own fruits.

With the growth of investigation has come the demand for better means of work, better apparatus, more and better books, larger collections, and especially collections for work, not for show or surprise. Better teachers are needed, and more of them. A healthy competition is set up, by which in these later days a man's pay is in some degree proportioned to his power, and the competition for places among half-starved men is changing into a competition for men among rich and ambitious institutions.

One of the great changes which have come to American education has been the extension of scientific methods to many subjects formerly deemed essentially unscientific. For this change the influences which have come to us from Germany are largely responsible. Thirty years ago the mental philosophy which formed the staple of the work of the college president was thoroughly dogmatic, like his moral science and his political economy. It was a completed subject, having its base in speculation and its growth by logical deductions, and no thought of experimental proof or of advancement by investigation was ever brought before the student.

Now psychology is completely detached from metaphysics, and is an experimental science as much as physiology or embryology. By its side ethics and pedagogics are ranging themselves — the scientific study of children and the study of the laws of right, by the same methods as those we use to test the laws of chemical affinity. Metaphysics, too, has ranged itself among the historical sciences. It is the study no longer of intuitive and absolute truth, but the critical investigation of the outlook of man on the universe, as shown through the history of the ages. The old metaphysical idea is passing away, soon to take its place with the science of the dark ages in which it rose.

History, too, is no longer a chronicle of kings and battles. It is the story of civilization, the science of human society and human institutions. The Germans have taught us that all knowledge is science, capable of being placed in orderly sequence, and of being increased by the method of systematic investigation.

The study of language now finds its culmination in the science of philology, the science of the growth of speech. Every branch of learning is now studied, or may be studied, inductively, and studied in the light of the conception of endless and orderly change, to which we give the name of evolution. This conception has come to be recognized as one underlying all human knowledge.

Seasons return because conditions return, but the conditions in the world of life never return. The present we know, but we can know it thoroughly only in the light of the past. What has been must determine what is, and the present is bound to the past by unchanging law. All advance in knowledge implies a recognition of this fact. The study of science must be grounded in the conception of orderly change, or change in accordance with the laws of evolution.

It is, after all, the presence of scholars that makes the university. It is in such men that the University of Illinois has its existence. It is located neither in Champaign nor in Urbana; it is wherever its teachers may be, wherever its workers have gone. We have met to-day to dedicate its science hall. To the future work in this hall we do all honor, but we do not think of it as a new hall, nor a new creation. It is simply a natural outgrowth of the work of Burrill and Forbes. Ever since, in 1878, I visited the little zoological workshop of Dr. Forbes in the old school building at Normal, and ever since, in 1882, I saw toadstools and bacteria in the little room across the way, which Dr. Burrill called his own, I have been able to prophesy the growth of this building. We care nothing for the brick building, its desks, its shelves, and its microscopes, as things in themselves. We are thinking of Forbes and Burrill. The building is only a better tool-house in which these master-workmen can shelter their tools. Their work will be what it was before. And in this impulse and example is our best guarantee that so long as this building stands we shall find in it master-workmen. Another Forbes, another Burrill, another Rolfe shall fill the gaps when these lay down their work, and the University of Illinois shall live through the years, because the men who compose it are truthful, devoted, and strong.

XIII.

THE PROCESSION OF LIFE.*

I ONCE walked one Saturday afternoon out from the city of Canterbury across the fields of Kent. The hops were ripe on the chalk hills; for the growing of hops is the chief industry in that part of England. The hop-pickers had finished their week's work and were returning to their homes in Canterbury for their Sunday rest. I walked out on the Gadshill road and met them on the way—a long, long procession of modern pilgrims. They came by hundreds and hundreds. There may have been five thousand of them in all. In the lead were the young and vigorous, the stalwart young man, the spirited young woman, those who thought nothing of a ten-mile walk when the day's work was over. Next came the older ones, equally strong, but more serious, who went on their way with an even step; while behind these, in the main body of the procession, were the old and the young, those whose strength was passing and those to whom strength had not yet come.

Then, behind the middle came those who had more than themselves to carry; men leading boys or girls, women with baskets, or with children who clung to their skirts. Still behind these were women carrying babies, and men limping on crutches. And, last of all, were men who had taken the burden of a load of gin from

* Address to graduating class, University of Indiana, 1890.

203

some wayside tavern; for the heaviest load a man can carry is the weight of a glass of liquor.

And the thought came to me, as I watched them, that this modern procession of pilgrims to Canterbury was but a fragment of a greater procession which moves before our eyes all our lives — the endless procession in which you who go from us to-day step forth to form a part. The thought of a Pilgrim's Progress, as it came to John Bunyan in the Bedford jail, is one which rises naturally as we look over the course of human life. What loads have we to carry, and how shall we come to our journey's end? We start with our burdens of hereditary weaknesses and hereditary sins, and to these we add many new ones which we take up along the road. What prospect have we of reaching Canterbury before the sun goes down? And of what avail are our efforts on the road if we never reach Canterbury?

Or, laying aside the metaphor, which may prove cumbersome, we meet the old question which comes afresh to every man, though countless generations have attempted its solution; what for us constitutes success in life? Certainly not the gaining of wealth, though many of our fellow-pilgrims seem to think so. If it were wealth alone, we have surely missed the way. You are not on the right road. There is a shorter way to wealth than the way you have taken, though the road may not lead to Canterbury. If you spend your day searching for gold, you will find it. A man finds whatever he goes forth to seek; but gold has no value except the value your fellow-pilgrims agree to set upon it — the worth of the time, we may say, they waste when they stop to look for it. When a man is alone with gold, he is alone with—nothing.

Not fame alone can constitute success. The gods care little for what men say of one another. Not the acquisition of power alone. The force of man can change nothing which is not already bound to change. A lever can move the world only when applied to a world which is moving. The force of man counts for nothing when placed in opposition to the laws of human development.

We are encompassed about by the forces that make for righteousness. All power we possess, or seem to possess, comes from our accord with these forces. There is no lasting force, except the power of God. All else in the world is speedily passing away. Is there no success for the individual? Are all lives alike ineffective? Not so. Measured by the standard of the Infinite, all life is short, and weak, and impotent; yet we know that, gauged by the measure of a man, there are many lives which are successful. We have all come in contact with such, and our own lives have been the richer for the contact. But we know, too, that there are broken lives. We pass them on the road. They stagger against us from the tavern steps. They are carried on for a time by the procession; but having no impulse of their own, they drop farther and farther behind — sometimes alone, sometimes dragging others with them.

These are not successful lives. What lessons do they teach? What have these broken lives in common? And what is this common element which we who hope for success can avoid? Is it poverty? Is life a failure if we gain not wealth, we who now live in the wealthiest of all times, here among the richest of all peoples?

There are many who think this. Poverty is pictured

as the yawning and relentless gulf beneath our whole civilization. If we avoid poverty, are we assured against all forms of spiritual failure?

We know that this is not true. Broken lives are as common among the rich as among the poor. In the palace and the hovel we may look for them alike. Chronic poverty may be a sign of a withered spirit, but it is not the cause. The real disease lies far behind this, as those know well who have tried to heal the sores of poverty by filling them with gold.

Poverty, in itself, is not even a cause for discouragement. Poverty has been through the ages the heritage of the student, and in the procession of life the student has never walked in the rear. You who stand before me, the flower of our student body, do not stand with well-filled purses. Your money and lands, to take the average, would not keep you for a single year. The inmates of many poorhouses could make a better actual showing than you could make to-day. Yet you are not paupers. No one dreams of thinking you such. You have something, not money, which helps you to face the future. And it is something real — something which has a quotable value. No; the element of likeness in broken lives is not their poverty.

Is it sickness or weakness which makes failure in life? We know that it is not. Stalwart frames stand all about us from which the spirit seems to have fled, while there are other souls whom no pain or disease can tame. The great name of the nineteenth century cannot be that of an unsuccessful man; yet for forty years of his earnest and beautiful life Darwin knew not a single day of health such as other men enjoy — not a single day such as

comes unasked and unappreciated to you and to me.
Health is much, but it is not everything. A withered
arm does not mean a broken spirit.

What then can we ask as our surety against failure?
That which we seek, does it not lie in the very heart of
man, the presence of a reason for living? Is not this
the one touchstone which through the ages has separated
success from failure in life? If a man live for worthy
ends, his life is made worthy. With a lifelong purpose,
and a purpose worthy of a life, there can be no failure.
How can there be? Be a life long or short, its completeness depends on what it was lived for.

Stand for something — something worthy to build a
life around. As your aim, so your life is. Your purpose,
like an amulet, will guard you from failure. While it
remains intact, your life cannot be broken. Poverty
cannot hold you down, disease cannot weaken, adversity
cannot crush. Your life remains, and you alone can
break it. It takes a strong impulse to live a life out to
the end. If you live to no true purpose, your life is a
burden on the atmosphere, and death will come to you
long before you even suspect it. All around you are
those who have died already — perhaps never have lived
at all. More terrible than ghosts or disembodied spirits
is the spectacle we see every day of spiritless bodies —
the forms of those who move and breathe when we know
them to be dead.

And so, when as year by year your paths diverge over
the earth, let us hope and pray, that you may live your
lives out to the end; that at every roll-call in this world,
when you answer to your names, it will be in the full certainty that you are still alive.

XIV.

THE GROWTH OF MAN.*

A WISE man once said, "The Bible was written by
outdoor men; if we would understand it, we must
read it out of doors." They were shepherds and fisher-
men who wrote the Bible; men who, night after night,
lay under the stars, and to whom the grass on the
Judæan hills had been the softest of pillows. Even kings
and prophets were out-of-door men in the days of Sam-
uel and David. Out-of-door men speak of out-of-door
things, and each man who speaks with authority must
speak of things which he knows.

In this fact, if you will let me compare small things to
great, you will find my apology for speaking my message to-day in my own way. I wish to draw certain
lessons in morals from certain facts, or laws, in the sciences of which I know something. For we study what
we call Nature, not for the objects themselves, but because the study brings us nearer to the heart of things,
nearer to the final answer to all the problems of death
and of life.

There is a stage in the development of the human
embryo when it is not yet human, when it cannot be distinguished from the embryo of other mammals, as of a
dog or a sheep. There may be, at the same time, two
embryos apparently alike, the one destined to be a dog,

* Commencement Address, University of Indiana, 1889.

208

because of its canine ancestry; the other, in like manner, to become human. These two, we may assume, may be absolutely alike to all the tests we can offer. They differ neither in structure, nor in form, nor in chemical composition. The lines along which they develop seem parallel for a time, but at last divergence becomes evident, and their courses separate forever. The one seems to lose, little by little, its human possibilities, while the other goes too far in its way ever to turn aside to doghood. The one moves toward its end as man; the other toward its destiny as dog.

But a difference must exist, even when the identity of the two seems most perfect — a difference intangible, immaterial, but none the less potent in its certainty to lead to results. The one embryo holds within it the possibility of humanity which the other has not. No conditions of which we can conceive will bring the dog embryo to manhood, because the possibility of manhood is not in it. There is something which transcends chemistry, which tends to bring each embryo through many changes to a predetermined end.

This is essentially true if the development be complete and normal. If its growth goes on in the wonted fashion, it becomes what it can become. Its enclosed potentiality, or hidden powers, give form to its life. But not all development is normal. Growth may cease prematurely, or it may be cut short by death, and that which might have been a man becomes as nothing; or arrested development may leave a state of perpetual immaturity. This happens among men sometimes. There are dwarfs in body and dwarfs in mind — those who reach the age of manhood while retaining the stature or the intellect of

o

children.   Again, decay and decline come sooner or
later to all living things.   If decline begins prematurely,
we have degeneration instead of development.   What is
true of man in these regards is true of all life in its degree; for there is no law of human development which
does not, in corresponding measure, apply to animals
and plants.

On the other hand, progress begets progress.   Naturalists tell us of cases of development beyond ancestral
lines, of perfection beyond previous completeness.   In
such growth, the conditions which mark full maturity in
the ancestor become phases of youth in the ambitious
progeny.   The maturity of the latter in one or more ways
overleaps ancestral lines.   Such advanced development
here and there through the organic world is one of the
causes of the progress of the mass.   By the side of the
philosopher the common man seems like a child.   The
development of great souls has gone on in accordance
with a higher potentiality than ours.   Or, rather, it may
be in accordance with a potentiality which we possess,
but which has lain dormant within us.   For great men
need great occasions.   Circumstances affect all development.   They may draw us out, or they may hem us in.
They may raise us, as it were, above ourselves, or they
may close around us, so that the man we ought to have
been we are only in our dreams.   And if the environment
be too exacting, even these dreams cease at last.

The lower animals and plants offer analogies to this.
Each individual develops along the line of the resultant
between the force of its own potentiality and the resist-
ance of its environment.   Thus, all degrees of fitness are
produced, and from these varying degrees comes our

perception of the law of the survival of the fittest in the struggle for existence. One of the primal causes of difference in organic life lies in the conditions of advanced or retarded development. A higher — that is, a more definitely developed — organism is one that has taken a step in its growth beyond those taken by its ancestors. It has omitted non-essential phases and has leaped at once to a higher range of its possibilities. It has come so much nearer the fulfillment of the potentialities within it. Another organism may stop short of ancestral acquirements. It is degenerate; for less of its potentiality has become actuality than in its ancestors.

Florists save the seed of their fairest flowers, that from these the species may reach still higher perfection. Stock-breeders recognize that individual gains are inherited, and they choose their stock accordingly. So we have, year by year, swifter race-horses, better milk cows, sheep with heavier fleece, more sagacious dogs, and pigeons of more fantastic forms. Along certain lines of development anything is possible with time and patience. Because this is so, with each generation our domestic animals and plants become better and better adapted to satisfy man's needs or man's fancy. But the potentiality of the race-horse was in the old nag, its far-off ancestor, who may have trotted his leisurely mile in ten minutes. The potentiality of the trained dog, "who can do anything but talk," lay in the gaunt and cowardly wolf, from which the races of dogs are descended.

More perfect development comes from within, and is assisted, not caused, by favorable surroundings. This is shown in the very terms we use. We *educate*—that is, we "lead out." We *develop*—that is, we "unwrap"

what was hidden in the original package.   We *evolve* —
that is, we "unroll," as the ball of the fern-bud unrolls
into the great fern leaf.   And so we *unroll, unwrap, lead
out* whatever is already within.   We can help to actualize
latent possibilities.   But whatever is finally brought forth
existed in potentiality in the embryo, no matter how
inert and impotent this may have been.   But not alone
in the embryo; for whatever is in the embryo must have
been a possibility with the parent.

No great thing comes from nothingness.   There must
have been strength behind it.   There must have been a
potential Lincoln in Lincoln's humble ancestry, else a
Lincoln could not have been.   We can trust that studies
in genealogy will some time show this.   In each life there
must exist a potentiality of something not yet attained.
Were it not so, the bounds of progress would be already
reached, and swifter horses, brighter flowers, sweeter
songs, nobler thoughts, and purer lives than have already
been there could never be.   Potentiality may be con-
ceived as a series of direct lines leading from the past
into the future, outward into space.   The highest potentiality is that one of these lines which most favors
fullness of life.   For any organism to grow along this
highest line is for it to make the most of itself — and the
most of its descendants, too; for the will to do the best
may fall into the grasp of heredity.   The gain of the
individual becomes the birthright of the race.   The man
of yesterday is a child beside the man of to-morrow.
Our ancestors of centuries ago dwelt beside the Swiss
lakes in children's playhouses.   Whatever one generation has tried persistently to do, the next may accomplish
easily.   If by effort we have, as it were, excelled our-

selves, our children may also without effort excel us in
the same line. The man we dream of will be above the
weaknesses of past humanity. The perfect man will be
the master of the world, because the perfect master of
himself.

As in the physical world there are many departures
from the normal type, there may be partial, distorted, or
degraded development. In the moral world the same
conditions exist; and such departures from the ideal
type we call sin. Sin is man's failure to realize his
highest possibilities. Its measure is the discrepancy
between the actual and the possible man. It is the
spiritual analogue of retrograde or distorted development. Personal degeneration is sin. Misery, in general,
is nature's protest against personal degeneration.

Total depravity is not the state of nature. It is the
good man who is natural; it is the weak and vicious who
are least human. "Great men are the true men," says
Amiel, "the men in whom nature has succeeded. They
are not extraordinary. They are in the true order. It
is the other kinds of men that are not what they ought
to be. If we wish to respect men, we must forget what
they are and think of the ideal they have hidden in them
— of the just man and the noble, the man of intelligence
and goodness, inspiration and creative force, who is loyal
and true,— of the higher man and that divine thing we
call soul. The only men who deserve the name are the
heroes, the geniuses, the saints, the harmonious, powerful, and perfect examples of the race."

If, then, sin is retarded or distorted development,
righteousness is further development along the line of our
ethical possibilities. Righteousness is thus achieved only

by constant effort in the direction of self-control and self-devotion. As Aristotle says, "Nature does not make us either good or bad; she only gives us the opportunity to become good or bad — that is, of shaping our own characters." "Emphasize as you will," says Dr. Schurmann, "the bulk of the inheritance I have received from my ancestors, it still remains that in moral character I am what I make myself." This is the higher heredity, the aggregate of all our own past actions or conditions; our deeds in the "vanished yesterdays that rule us absolutely." "On stepping-stones of their dead selves do men rise to higher things." And in a similar way, on stepping-stones of their ancestry, do races of men rise to higher civilization. But without effort, conscious or unconscious, in the direction of a higher life, each succeeding generation will fail to rise above the level of those before it. Then, as nothing is stable in the world of life, where there is no advance there will be retrogression. And thus have fallen all races, and nations, and communities whose guiding principle has not been the fulfillment of duty.

If there be any truth at the basis of these analogies, they are susceptible of wide application to the affairs of human life.

The central thought of modern biology is that all life is bound together by heredity, the ancestry of all beings going back with gradual changes through countless ages to simpler and simpler forms. Connected with this is the fact that the various stages in the development of an embryo correspond essentially with the conditions of full development in the creatures which, one before another, have preceded its appearance in geological history.

"The physical life of the individual is an epitome of the history of the group to which it belongs." The embryonic life of the child corresponds in a general way to the history of the group which culminates in man. The stages in the mental development of the child of this century represent roughly the stages passed through in the infancy of our race. In this sense each life is a condensation of the history of all life. "In every grave," says the German proverb, "lies a world's history."

From our study of evolution arises the new science of ethics, which teaches what ought to be from the knowledge of what has been. " Time was, unlocks the riddle of Time is." The central question in this study cannot be, as some have said, " what in the past man has thought ought to be," but what in the past has justified itself by leading man on to higher things. We can discover traces of the path which humanity shall tread, by looking backward over the road humanity has trodden. not alone over the early history of man; for only the smaller portion of this is within our reach. Our history of man is only a history of civilization; for barbarism writes no history, We can look beyond the clouded period of human barbarism to the still older history which we share with the brute. If we find the line of direction of past development from animalism to civilization, we may in a way project this line into the future as the direction of human progress.

What is this line of direction? How does man differ from the brute?

The intellect of man is certainly a distinctive possession. It is not necessary, as has been said, "to deny intelligence to the lower animals when we assert that the human mind is the most colossal and revolutionary of all the modifications any species has undergone." It is not necessary to deny the elements of conscience to a dog or a horse in recognizing the fact that conscience is one of the essential attributes of manhood. The feeling of individual responsibility, the knowledge of good and evil — this is man's burden and his glory. Intellect and conscience — these are the acquisitions won by humanity, and by virtue of which it is humanity.

This thought need not prevent our recognition of the natural origin of these powers; for all phenomena are alike natural. The simple automatic reflex action in which the psychic force of the lower animals expresses itself is unquestionably the prototype of all nervous processes. Sensation — thought — action : this is the only order in which these phenomena can arise. The senses are the only source of action. All thought tends to pass over into deeds, and no mental process is complete until it has wrought itself into action. The brain has no teacher save the sensory nerves, which bring it knowledge. Its only servant is the muscles, for by their agency alone can it reach the outside world. In its essence, the intellect is the ability to choose among many possible responses in action. Simple reflex action, or "instinct," has no choice. It acts automatically, and in its one unchanging way. To choose one act rather than another is an intellectual process. This power of choice brings its responsibilities. Whoever chooses must choose aright. Wrong choice carries its own destruction. The conscience is the recognition, more or less automatic, that some lines of choice are better than others, and must be followed. By "better," in this connection, we must mean favoring life. That is best that "brings life more abundantly." That is best which brings self-realization to the individual and to his fellows. In social life, self-seeking is not "right," even for the individual. For the welfare of the one is bound up in the welfare of all. Here arises the ever-present problem of the conciliation of the claims of oneself and the claims of others. To solve this problem is part of the work of the rational life. All right must be relative. It may be compared to a line of direction rather than a position in space. There can be no absolute righteousness. If there were, it would mark the limit of spiritual growth.

To show the origin of conscience by the natural processes of development and competition in life is not to deny its existence or to lower its importance. All things we know are natural alike — the creation of man, or the formation of a snow-bank. All are alike supernatural; for the nature we know is not the whole of nature. Any fact or process becomes exalted when we see it in its true relation, as inherent in the nature of things. Right conduct, so Emerson tells us, is "conformity in action to the nature of things, and the nature of things makes it prevalent." The automatic or rational recognition of the fact that one response is better than another is an attribute of man. The stronger the conscience of man or race, the higher its place in the scale of spiritual development. The conscience is the real essence of that "something not ourselves that makes for righteousness." For that "something," though "not ourselves," has its seat in the nature of man. The fulfillment of the noblest possibilities of the individual — that is right.

What falls short of this is arrest of development, imperfection, sin.

The conscience no more than any other group of mental processes can claim infallibility. It may be distorted, dormant, ineffective. A "clear" conscience is of itself the result of normal development. Arrested development is none the less a fault that its subject is not aware of it. Nature absolves no sinner on the plea of ignorance of her laws. The bent twig is none the less bent that outside influences have done the bending. The tree should have grown upright, and in this it has failed.

It is often said that conscience is only relative; that what is right to-day will be wrong to-morrow, and there can be no absolute good but the pleasure or the utility of the individual. What is the truth of this? Let us take for illustration the customs and laws of marriage. The patriarchs of old did wrong, so the chronicles tell us; but neither the patriarchs nor their prophets, scathing moralists though these were, counted the possession of many wives as even the least of their wrong-doings. The sin of David lay not in taking another wife, but in the murder which gave him possession of her. Our civilization now condemns polygamy, and our statutes and beliefs tend to exalt the sanctity and the unity of the home. Is marriage for life but a fashion of the time, to pass away as polygamy has done, when opposite tendencies have sway? Is the one really right, and the other really wrong? What tests can we apply to this question?

It can be shown, I think, that the richest human life is dependent upon the development of the home. The elevation of woman has been the keystone in modern social development. The ennobling of the wife and mother means the elevation of the race. And the elevation of woman is impossible in polygamy. If this be true, the highest potentiality of the race can be brought about only through the marriage of the equal man with the equal woman. It may be literally true that polygamy, wife-beating, wife-selling, and similar practices were right in the infancy of the race. They may be right among races still in their infancy. "It is their condemnation that light has come into the world." They may be part of a stage of growth through which humanity must pass before higher things are possible.

In like manner, we have gone through a slow process of development in our regard for the rights of others. To the lower animals, each other animal is an alien and an enemy. A little higher in the scale we observe the rudiments of family, or social, life; yet, in a general way, to the brute all other brutes are objects of suspicion and hatred. The earlier tribes of men killed the stranger, and doubtless ate him, too, with perfect serenity of conscience. Even the most enlightened nation of ancient times murdered and robbed all alien to their race, as a high and sacred duty toward the Lord. Their God was a god of battles.

Every foot of soil in Europe bears the stain of blood wantonly shed. There is not a moment in its history but has been marked by some cry of anguish. The history of the Old World has been one long story of needless suffering and needless waste. Yet the wave of brutality has been an ever-receding tide. With each century it rises never so high again. We have seen the last

St. Bartholomew, the last Bloody Assizes, and perhaps the
last Waterloo and the last Sedan. The old house ''in
Duizend Vreezen,'' the house of the ''thousand terrors,''
on the marketplace of Rotterdam, stands as a memorial
of what can never happen again. Human life is growing
sacred. The history of civilization is a story of the
growth of kindness and tolerance among men.

The history of slavery teaches us the same lesson.
Once to enslave a conquered enemy was to treat him
with comparative kindness. Slavery is a positive advance
from cannibalism, or from massacre. We find no condemnation of slavery in the early history of the Jews.
We find none in the early history of Europe. Slaves
have been bought and sold in our country by strong,
pure men, who felt no rebuke of conscience. The heroes
of the Revolutionary history were not abolitionists.

Yet it is true, ''for the Lord hath said it,''* that the
man of the future will not be a slave-holder. There
can be no free men in a land where some are slaves,
because whatever oppression comes to my neighbor in
some sort comes to me. ''He hath made of one
blood all the nations of the earth,'' and '' Whatsoever

---

* This metaphor may find its justification in the lines of Maurice Thomp-
son:

—'' I am a Southerner.
I love the South. I dared for her
To fight from Lookout to the Sea
With her proud banner over me.
But from my lips thanksgiving broke
When God in battle thunder spoke,
And that black idol, breeding drouth
And dearth of human sympathy,
Throughout the sweet and sensuous South,
Was, with its chains and human yoke
Blown hellward from the cannon's mouth
While Freedom cheered behind the smoke.''

ye do to one of the least of these my brethren, ye do it unto me."

We know that humanity is growing toward the recognition of the need of equal opportunity for all men and women. The cardinal doctrine of democracy is "Equal rights for all, exclusive privileges to none." This is the tendency of human institutions. "We hold these truths to be self-evident," said our fathers a century ago, "that all men are created free and equal, endowed with certain inalienable rights, and that among these rights are life, liberty, and the pursuit of happiness." And these rights cannot be denied, even though the image of God shine faintly through a dusky skin.

The feeling of brotherhood is extending to the brute creation. A society for "the prevention of cruelty to animals" would have been inconceivable in the days of Front-de-Bœuf or of Cœur-de-Lion. It is inconceivable now in those countries which are a century or two behind our race in the march of civilization. In the city of Havana, in the early morning, long lines of mules laden with pigs and sheep come in from the country. These animals' legs are bound, and they are slung head downward, in pairs saddlewise, over the back of a mule. Thus they come down from the mountains in long processions, the pigs lustily squealing, the sheep helpless and dumb. No one notes their suffering; for in Cuba no one seems to care for an animal's pain. On Sunday afternoons in the same city of Havana, fair ladies and gay cavaliers repair to the brightest of their festivals, the bull-fight. A bull-fight is not a fight; it is simply a butchery; a fair battle has some justification. The bull, maddened by pricks and stabs, is permitted to rip up and kill some two or three feeble or blind horses, to be afterwards stabbed to death himself by a skillful butcher. A civilization which delights in scenes like this is to us simple barbarism. The growth of the race is away from such things. Cruelty to animals may not have been wrong when the race was undeveloped, and no conscience enlightened enough to condemn it. Cruelty in all its forms is a badge of immaturity, and toward neither man nor beast will the ideal man of the future be cruel. With time the feeling of brotherhood will extend to all living things, so far as community of sensation makes them akin to us.

We cannot tell how far this feeling of brotherhood must go. This is certain, that our present relation toward animals, right as they may be now, will some day be barbarous. It may be that the time will come when the civilized man will feel that the rights of every living creature on the earth are as sacred as his own. This end may be far away, too far for us even to dream of it; but anything short of this cannot be perfect civilization.

" If man were what he should be," says Amiel, " he would be adored by the lower animals, toward whom he is too often the capricious and sanguinary tyrant. A day will come when our standard will be higher, our humanity more exacting. ' *Homo homini lupus,*' said Hobbes, ' man toward men is a wolf.' The time will come when man will be humane, even toward the wolf — ' *homo lupo homo.*' "

No fact in Jewish history stands out more clearly than that of the gradual growth of the law of love. " An eye for an eye, a tooth for a tooth "—even this marks a great advance over the ethics of the Ammonites and the

children of Heth. Yet between this and the Sermon on
the Mount lies the whole difference between barbarism
and the highest civilization.

" Ye have heard that it hath been said, Thou shalt love thy
neighbor and hate thine enemy; but I say unto you, Love your
enemies; bless them that curse you; do good to them that hate
you."

" But dig down, the old unbury, thou shalt find on every stone
That each age has carved the symbol of that God to them was
    known.
Ugly shapes and brutish sometimes; but the fairest that they
    knew;
If their sight were dim and earthward, yet their hope and aim
    were true.
As the gods were, so their laws were, Thor the strong might
    rave and steal,
So through many a peaceful inlet tore the Norseman's eager
    keel.
But a new law came when Christ came, and not blameless as
    before,
Can we, paying Him our lip-tithes, give our lives and faiths to
    Thor."

This question, then, is ours — Are we doing our part
in the growth of the race? In the current of life are we
moving forward? Do our years mark milestones in
humanity's struggle toward perfection? Is the god
within us so much the more unrolled, when our development has reached its highest point? Can we transmit to
our children a better heritage of brain and soul than our
fathers left to us? Has the race through us gained some
little in the direction of the law of love? If we have
done our part in this struggle, our lives have not been in
vain. If we have shirked and hung back, then ours is a

line of retrograde descent, and our lineage is a withered branch on the tree of humanity.

To live aright, is to guide our lives in the direction in which humanity is going — not all humanity, not average humanity, but that saving remnant from whose loins shall spring the better man of the future. The purpose of life is to be as near the man of the future as the man of the present can be. But we must be patient, with all our striving. The end of life is not yet. Humanity is still in its infancy, and this old world is old only in comparison with the years of human life. Only through centuries on centuries of struggle and aspiration can humanity approach divinity and the law of love be supreme.

Books have been written on the seven or eight "decisive battles" in the history of civilization. Great battles there have been; but the stake in any battle is less than it appears. There can have been no decisive battles. The growth in humanity goes on whether battles be lost or won. The leaven of Christianity would have wrought its work in Europe if Charles Martel had been overpowered by the Moors at Poitiers. A battle may decide the fate of a man or a nation, but not the fate of humanity. Kings cannot check its growth. Priests cannot smother it. It is never buried in the dust of defeat.

Slavery died not because the battle of Gettysburg was lost. It was doomed from the beginning, and its death was only a question of time. Nothing could have saved it, and the success of its defenders on the field of battle would only have postponed the end. The forces of nature are fatal to it. Even the law of gravitation and the multiplication-table would have conquered it at last. That which endures is that which brings out the higher potentialities of manhood. All else must pass away.

Not long ago, in a gallery in Brussels, I saw that striking painting of Wiertz, "The Man of the Future and the Things of the Past." The man of the future has in his open right hand a handful of marshals, guns, swords, and battle-flags, the paraphernalia of Napoleon's campaigns. These he is carefully examining with a magnifying-glass which he holds above them in his left hand. At the same time a child beside him looks on in open-eyed wonder that a man should care so much for such little things as these. For these banners and arms, so potent in their day, dwindle to the proportions of children's toys when seen in the long perspective of human development.

The decline and fall of empires is not decline or decay. It is the breaking of the clods above the growing man. Kings and nations recede as man moves on. The love of country must merge into the higher patriotism, the love of man. Viewed as steps in the growth of ascending humanity, the changes in history have a deeper meaning to us. Our studies become ennobled. What have been the conditions of growth in the past? What conditions have led to decline and degradation? What tends to keep the individual retarded and immature, and what tends to bring him farther toward the ultimate humanity?

Now, as we look back over the annals of slowly advancing humanity, and behold the gradual development in wisdom, skill, self-control, and kindness can we not also look forward along the same line to a future of

P

ideal manhood? If Christ be the perfect man, He is perfect in this, that the potentiality of the race finds its fulfillment in Him. Seen in contrast with the perfect humanity, all else that we know is but infantile. Decay and death overtake us long before we begin to realize any appreciable nearness to the sublime ideal of the Christian faith.

"*De Imitatione Christi*" is one of the grand books of the middle ages. "Imitation of Christ," so far as the imitation is real — not in speech, not in dress, not in ceremonies, but in the inner life, — this alone can place us in close harmony with nature, and closer with our fellow-men. The expression, "love of God," is the love of good, the love of that which is abiding, in distinction from that which is merely temporal. It may reduce itself into love of the higher life, in which the progress of the race consists. For, in the words of the good Thomas à Kempis, "It is vanity to love that which is speedily passing away." In the despairing words of Guinevere may be heard the keynote of the conditions of growth:

"It was my duty to have loved the highest!"

"This is the first and great commandment. And the second is like unto it. Thou shalt love thy neighbor as thyself. On these two commandments hang all the law and the prophets."

What I have tried to say, I may sum up in a few words. There is an ideal manhood to which our human race must come. Every step toward this end which the individual man may take is a step won for humanity. The end rests with us. It is our part in life to work with all our strength toward the realization of ideal humanity, to add one more link to the chain which joins the man-brute of the past through the man of the present to the man of the future — the man who is likest Him we have chosen for our ideal.

XV.

THE SOCIAL ORDER.*

IN the crude civilization of to-day there is no place for
anarchy. Order is more important than even freedom, and order must be upheld by force if it cannot be
maintained in any other way. Yet the ideal of civilization must be perfect anarchy — order maintained from
within, the recognition of order in the hearts of men;
not order imposed upon men from without, but the
forces within that make for righteousness of thought
and action. The fruitage of civilization must be voluntary co-operation. When this fruitage is reached, then
it will be time for us to cast aside our present social
order, to organize a new one adapted to the changed
human nature of the coming time, if indeed the new one
by that time is not already formed and adopted uncon-
sciously and in spite of ourselves. We have been
thousands of years working out the social order we have.
It is the best that man has ever found; it is the best that
has been possible with the weak and wayward men who
are the units of civilization. It is easy to find fault with
our present social organization. Like the men of whom
it is made, it has thousands of crimes to answer for. It
has been the chief of the "plug-uglies." It has ground
slaves into the dust and murdered those who would be
their liberators. In the name of law it still daily defies

* Notes from an unpublished lecture.

228

all law. It daily stands, and must stand, for injustice and
oppression, but it also stands for the removal of injustice
and oppression, for the growth of knowledge, the lessen-
ing of crime, the bringing of freedom to the oppressed,
of wisdom to the foolish, of help to the unfortunate. It
has throughout the ages been in advance of the men
from whom it arises and of whom it is composed. Its
movement is not the expression of the best in man.
That could not be, for society is collective. Nor is it
the expression of the worst, nor even of the average. It
is better than the average, for this reason — that a good
man has more weight in society and more force in himself than a bad one; a strong man counts for more than
a weak one, a wise man for more than a fool; and this
will always be so.

The perfect anarchy will not come through dynamite.
Dynamite is the weapon of a coward. The men who,
by deeds of violence, have broken systems or shaken
society have been the men who have given their own
lives as a sacrifice, not the men who have given the lives
or property of their neighbors. Such men as these
have not needed to fortify themselves with stimulants
nor with the enthusiasm or the cheers of others. It was
not the courage of whisky that brought John Brown to
the gallows nor John Huss to the stake. These men
had no need to manufacture dynamite bombs or to kill
the burghers that their influence might be felt. They
gave themselves as a sacrifice to an unjust statute or an
unjust decree, that people might learn to see clearly the
difference between these and the laws of God. These
laws have their basis, not in legislation, not in the statutes

of Congress, but in the very center of human nature, and can never be overthrown. Against law neither bullets nor ballots avail anything. But in mere statutes there is no force. Statutes are the manners and customs; law is the life itself. It is the expression of the onward movement of human civilization. A statute is a temporary compromise between struggling wills and jarring interests. It is the expression of the "patched-up broils of Congress." Through forms of statute men play at government, and in the long run in human development statutes count for nothing. Government by the people can be successful only as it becomes in time goverment by law, and not by statute.

The very perfection of society must always appear as imperfection; for a highly developed society is dynamic. It is moving on. A static society, no matter how perfect it may seem, whether a Utopia, Icaria, or City of the Sun, is in a condition of arrested development. Its growth has ceased and its perfection is that of death. The most highly advanced social conditions are the most unstable. The individual man counts for most under such conditions; for the growth of the individual man is the only justification for the institutions of which he forms part. The most highly developed organism shows the greatest imperfections. The most perfect adaptation to conditions needs readaptation, as conditions themselves speedily change. The dream of a static millennium, when struggle and change shall be over, when all shall be secure and all happy, finds no warrant in our knowledge of man and the world. Self-realization in life is only possible when self-perdition is also possible.

When cruelty and hate are excluded by force, charity and helpfulness will go with them. Strength and virtue have their roots within man, and not without. They may be checked but not greatly stimulated by institutions and statutes.

Thoreau tells us that, "as a snowbank rises when there is a lull in the wind, so when there is a lull in the truth an institution springs up. By and by, the truth blows on and sweeps it away." This truth which sweeps away institutions comes in the growth of the individual man. As his knowledge increases it is translated into action. In adapting himself to his environment, that which was the work of his own ignorance is swept away. By this means he is sometimes helpless, as the the lobster who has shed his shell. But the new shell he has formed, and which later he must likewise shed, is ever stronger and more roomy.

In making their own statutes the people come dimly to see that there is a power behind and above their efforts — the power of the nature of man. Hence, slowly as the experiment of self-government goes on, the rule of the people changes from folly to wisdom, from caprice to principle, from selfishness to justice, from statute to law. This is the expression of the growth of civilization. It is the essence of government by public opinion. It is the justification of universal suffrage. Universal suffrage is the expression of the growth of civilization, its extension downward, from rank to rank, from caste to caste — or, rather, from individual to individual. Thus "freedom slowly broadens down, from precedent to precedent." Each generation of men is as free as its character and training allows it to be. Each man has the rights he has the strength and wisdom to hold.

Any mistake in statutes is followed always by going farther in the same direction. The harm done by statutes based on unemotional reasoning is nothing to the mischief due to unreasoning emotion. The man who refuses to reason is always sure to be wrong. Emotion is not virtue — not always on speaking terms with it. "Virtue is more dangerous than vice, because its excesses are unchecked by conscience," says a French writer. The most dangerous of moral ideas are those held by men without intellectual ideas.

All goodness, all special helpfulness, is in some sense sacrifice, though this sacrifice may be recompensed in other ways. Men must be good if they are to live in society; that is, they must be considerate —"in honor preferring one another." But the virtues of men governments cannot have. A government cannot be good; it can simply be just; for government can sacrifice nothing. If it attempts to be kind as to the property and interests of others in one case, injustice results in other cases. Justice demands with all force that one set of interests shall not be sacrificed to another. Enforced sacrifice of the interests of others is not virtue, but injustice. Goodness must throw away self. The sacrifice must be self-sacrifice. Goodness enforced by law is corruption and injustice.

Society seems to exist for its own sake, but it does not. It exists for the sake of the individuals; but whenever society is imperiled, or in a struggle against its enemies, it must appear as a thing in itself. We must save our country in order to save ourselves.

All changes in human society and government must be dictated by wisdom, and actions must be right and wise. Hence the failure of the temperance movement and the populist movement as political attempts, because they are based on feeling, and on no scientific appreciation of the laws which determine what should be done, and what can be done. Good intentions do not rescue unwise actions from failure. A man of the best intentions is not always a good driver of an unruly team.

The growth of man means the decline of the machinery to control or to help him. He does not need governing when he has self-control. If he continuously needs special help, he is not a man, but a weakling or a degenerate. To give help at special times, for special needs, is part of the duty of altruism. All children are weaklings for the time being. They should be trained — never too much if wisely. But when full-grown, a man must give and take — give his power, and take the results of his actions. "To save men from the consequences of their folly," says Spencer, "is to fill the world with fools."

By good or right in human development, we mean simply the opportunity for more life or higher life. That is good which makes me strong and gives strength to my

neighbors.   Might does not make right; but whatever
is right will justify itself in persistence; and persistence
is strength.   That which is weak dies.   We only know
God's purposes by what He permits.   That which per-
sists and grows, must be in line with such purposes.   A
law is only an observed generalization of what is.   There
is no law which reads, "This and this ought to be, but
is not."

The law of God is different from the ordinances framed
in His name by bands calling themselves His servants.
His law has binding force from eternity to eternity.   The
decrees of the church extend only to the bounds of its
own vestry.   The statutes of the state have validity only
when its armies can secure their enforcement.

A parable of the conduct of life shows man in a light
skiff in a tortuous channel, beset with rocks, borne by a
falling current to an unknown sea.   He is kept awake
by the needs of his situation.   As his boat bumps against
the rocks, he must bestir himself.   If this contact were
not painful, he would not heed it.   If it were not hurtful,
he would not need to heed it.   Had he no power to act,
he could not heed it if he would.   But with sensation,
will, and the impulse to act, narrow though the range
of freedom of action may be, his safety rests in some
degree in his own hands.   That he has secured safety
thus far is shown by the fact that he is alive.   He may
choose his course for himself — not an easy thing to do,
unless he scans most carefully the nature of rocks and
waves, and his control of the boat itself.   He may follow
the course of others with some degree of the safety

that others have attained. He may follow his own impulses, the incentives those before him found safe as guides to action. But in new conditions neither conventionality, nor impulse, nor desire will suffice. He must know what is about him in order that he may know what he is doing. He must know what he is doing in order to do anything effectively. Blind action is more dangerous than no action at all. He must be in friendly relations with others, if for no other reason than that mutual help may bring a safety which no one could secure for himself alone. Wisdom is knowing what should be done next. Virtue is doing it. The will is man in action. The intellect is its guide. If the life of man, as thus pictured, be a life hemmed in by the inexorable Fates, then the Will is one of the Fates, and must take its place with the rest of them. The man who can will is a factor in the universe.

XVI.

THE SAVING OF TIME.*

"THE gods for labor give us all good things." This was part of the philosophy of the ancient Greeks. They learned it as a fact of experience long before Epicharnus first put it into words. Over and over again each generation of men tries its own experiments, and comes back to the same unvarying conclusion. In a thousand forms, in all languages, this idea has found its way into the wisdom of men. And it is a part of the same experience that the gods never give anything worth having for any other price. In their dealings with men they receive no other coinage. They know no other measure of value. Temporary loans they sometimes grant, but when the day of payment comes, they do not fail to charge their due rate of interest. They never change their valuations, and they never forget.

"By their long memories the gods are known." This proverb, like the other, has its source in a universal experience. Taken from the forms of classic poetry and cast into the language of to-day, it indicates simply the universality of law. When they spoke of the gods in phrases like these, the Greeks meant what we, in a different way, personify as the "Forces of Nature." These are the powers about us which act unceasingly, and in ways which never change. These are the realities

* Commencement Address, University of Indiana, 1891.

of the universe. All else is inert matter. Human knowledge consists in the recognition of these ways and forces.
We learn to know them from our contact with them.
Human power depends on acting in accord with such
knowledge. In this lie the possibilities of man. He
who knows the truth can trust all and fear nothing.
There is no treachery in Nature's laws. He who strikes
as the gods strike has the force of infinity in his blows.
He who defies them wields a club of air.

These laws are real and universal, and no man nor
nation has ever accomplished anything in opposition to
them. The existence of the simplest of these laws, those
which, like the law of gravitation, can be exactly determined, men now readily admit. The man who leaps from
a precipice expects to be hurt when he reaches the earth.
The law of falling bodies is too obvious to leave room for
doubt as to its results. But the laws of organic life are
less simple than these. The laws we but half understand
we hope in some way to defeat. Most complex of all
laws are those of ethics and economics. Because these
are not well understood, and the relations of cause and
effect are not easily traced, the average man believes that
he is shrewd enough to break them and to escape the
penalty.

One of these laws of life which men are prone to dis-
regard is that which decrees failure to him who seeks
something for nothing, and well-being to him who pays
as he goes.

It is one of the truths of modern biology that progress
in organic life comes through self-activity. In the last
analysis most forms of advance in power or in specialization of structure among organisms reduces itself to the

saving of time. Time must be measured in terms of
effort, and the essence of progress is that none should
slip by without effort or change.

In the embryonic stages of the various animal forms
there is a period when any two, higher and lower, are
alike; in this, at least, that no tests we may apply can
show a difference. One element of divergence comes
through the varying rates of developments. Time is saved
in the one organism; it is lost in the other. As growth
goes on, the forms we call lower pass slowly through
the various stages of life; their growth is altogether
finished before any high degree of specialization is
reached. The embryo of the higher form passes through
the same course, but with a swiftness in some degree
proportioned to its future possibility. Less time is spent
on non-essentials, and we may say that, through the
saving of time and force, it is enabled to push on to
higher development.

The gill structure of the fish, its apparatus for purify-
ing the blood by contact with the air dissolved in water,
lasts for its whole lifetime. In most fishes there is no
hint that any other mode of respiration could exist, or
could be effective. The frog, a higher animal than the
fish, sustains for part of its life a similar apparatus, but a
further development sets in, and at last the inherited
structure of the gills gives place to organs which insure
the contact of the blood with atmospheric air. Gill structures are likewise inherited by the bird, and mammal,
and man, as well as by the frog and fish; for by the law
of heredity no creature can ever wholly let go of its past.
The fact that its ancestors once breathed in water can
never be entirely forgotten. The same stages of growth

are passed through in birds or mammals as in frogs or fishes, but long before the bird is hatched or the mammal is born, the gill structures have disappeared, or have suffered total modification. The true life of the new animal is begun at a point far beyond the highest attainment of the frog or the fish. The law of acceleration hurries the embryo along through these temporary stages, and in this fact of acceleration comes the possibility of progress.

On the other hand, with animal or plant, degeneration and degradation result from the loss of time. Retarded development is incomplete development. Whatever narrows the activity of the individual, whatever tends to make of life — be it of animal or man — simply a matter of eating and sleeping and a continuance of the species, leads to degradation and loss of effectiveness. The creatures which rule the world are the children of struggle and storm. The sheltered life leads to inability to live without shelter. The loss of self-activity makes parasites and paupers, whether among animals, or plants, or men. It is one of those universal laws which act through all ages and all organisms, through the long memories of all the gods, that the creature which does not translate time into growth shall drop out of existence.

And now, leaving the lower orders of life aside, I wish to consider some relations of these laws of self-activity to our own lives and the lives of our neighbors. " A nation," it has been wisely said, "is an assemblage of men and women who can take care of themselves." Whatever influence strengthens this power in the individual makes the nation strong; and, conversely, the presence of every man or woman who does not, or can-

not, take care of himself, casts an additional burden on
the rest. This power of self-support goes with the saving
of the individual time. Franklin calculated that if every
man and woman should spend three or four hours each
day in useful occupation, poverty would disappear, and
the afternoon of each day and the whole afternoon of our
lives could be reserved for physical, mental, or spiritual
improvement. That we cannot thus have the afternoon
to ourselves is due to the fact that we are paying our
neighbor's debts. Our neighbor has taken our time.
We are doing more than our share of the drudgery that
hinders growth, and this because others in the same
community are doing too little for their own development.

The end of the social organism is fullness of life for the
individual. The forms of society avail nothing if they do
not bring larger life to the individual units. Whatever
is not good for the individual man, cannot be good for
humanity.

We hear every day allusions to the wrongs of labor,
to the justice which never comes to the poor man, and
to the favor which always follows the rich. We hear
of the industrial crimes by which the rich grow richer and
the poor grow poorer. We see every day the advertisements of the poor man's friend, paid for out of the poor
man's money, and all of them seem to tell the same
story. It is the desire of the poor man's friend to
handle the poor man's money, and his chief qualification is the fact that he has never yet shown any skill in
handling his own.

We know very well that these wrongs of labor are not
imaginary. It happens too often that those who are

within may bar tne doors against those who are without.
We know, too, that under human laws it too often occurs
that those the world calls fortunate have the luck of foxes
and wolves, and can show no moral claim to the game
they are devouring.

Much that we call money-making is not the addition
of wealth. It is money-transferring, not money-gaining.
It is the process of making slaves of others, by turning
into the pocket of the one that which is rightfully earned
by the brains or the hands of others. Some day this
manner of "making money," whether practiced by the
"predatory rich," or the equally "predatory poor,"
will become impossible. It will pass under the ban as
blackmail and highway robbery have passed. When it
is condemned by public opinion the law will condemn it,
too; for our statutes are only attempts at the formal
expression of such opinion. Industrial warfare is not
competition. It is the struggle of devices to stifle competition. Competition is rivalry, to be sure, but rivalry
under conditions of fair play. Its function is to secure
the best service — to put the right man in the right
place. That one man should devour another is not
competition. It is war. The abolition of private warfare
within a nation has been one of the most important steps
in human civilization. The abolition of private war in
industrial relations will be another step scarcely lower in
importance. But this must come with the growth of
human wisdom, by which destructive and dishonest practices may be condemned. It cannot be brought about by
the application of force. It cannot follow any form of
arbitrary legislation. All statutes must be of equal application; for in taking away from the barons, of whatever

Q

kind — feudal or industrial, — the right of private war, the people are bound to guarantee that private war shall not be waged against them.

With all that may be said of the injustice of our social order, there are not many whose place in it is not fixed by their own character and training.   In America to-day most men find that the position awarded them is the only one possible.   Accident and misfortune aside, not many are poor who could ever have been otherwise.   To Robinson Crusoe alone on his desert island, as Dr. Warner has shown, most forms of misery we know could have come if he had developed their causes.   Weakness and poverty are not wholly caused by social condi- tions.   Even with no social system at all, folly, vice, or crime will always bring weakness, misery, poverty. Misery, in general, is nature's protest against personal degradation.   No man needs the help of others in order to degrade himself.

To be poor in worldly goods is not all of poverty. Such poverty may be in itself no evil.   Wealth is a costly thing.   Many a man is poor because he has intelligently refused to pay the price of wealth.   He has turned his time and effort into channels which brought him spiritual or mental rather than economic gain.   But such as these are satisfied with their bargain, and not one of them is aware that any wrong has been done to him. He has what he has paid for, and asks for nothing else ; and we who know him as our neighbor never think of him as poor.   He could only wish for wealth as a means of securing a more perfect poverty.

" The gods for labor give us all good things," but not all to the same man.   Each must choose for himself, and it is a happy condition that each one who has earned the right to choose is satisfied with his choice. Those who have not earned this right must, from the nature of things, be discontented. The man who has wasted his time must take the last choice. He comes in for the little that is left. With the leisure of life all spent in advance, the interest on borrowed time must be paid under the hardest of creditors.

A great problem of our day, which engages the best thoughts of the strongest minds, is this: How can the power of self-support be restored to those who have lost it? How are those who swim on the crest of the wave to lend a hand to the submerged tenth who struggle ineffectively in waters which only grow deeper as our civilization moves on? What can the strong do for the weak?

"The rich man," it is often said, "must know how the poor man lives," for in keeping together is the safety of humanity. But even more pertinent than this is the other saying, that, in his turn, "the poor man must learn to know how the rich man works." It is true enough that there are among us some rich men who never work, some few supported splendidly in idleness, at public cost, the reward of the good fortune, or the hard work, or the successful trickery of some ancestor. These gilded paupers are not many in America, after all, — some "four hundred," are there not, in each of our great cities? And the number is not increasing; for their hold on inherited power grows constantly weaker. They are but froth on the waves of humanity, and the burden of carrying them is not one of the heaviest the American citizen has to bear. Their life in our country is an anachronism, as they themselves are not slow to recognize. Their place, and their time, is in feudal Europe, and not in the America of to-day.

In the old times the poor man worked, and the rich man was idle; the poor man paid the taxes which supported the gentleman in pauperism. "The rich," indeed, "grew richer, and the poor poorer." The poor man worked on with an ever-decreasing vitality, because work absorbed his strength, and he could not direct his own forces. Work without self-consent is not growth, but slavery. In like manner, the rich man slipped into degeneracy, because his existence was purposeless, and he was conscious of no need of self-support. The man of leisure, whether rich or poor, is in the body politic like carbonic acid in the air — it supports neither combustion nor respiration. His presence is poisonous, though in himself he may be productive of neither harm nor good.

There are some rich men, however, who have the right to be rich. They have paid the price, and they are entitled to enjoy their bargain. He who saves the toil of a thousand men has a right to some share of their earnings. Sooner or later, we may be sure, this share will be no more and no less than has been fairly earned. The forces of nature are hemmed in by no patent. No man can have a perpetual monopoly; and, sooner or later, the knowledge of the one becomes the property of all.

The power of capital does not lie in its own force, but in the force of the brains which must, sooner or later, take possession of it, and to which labor undirected by mind must ever stand in the relation of a slave. Money alone has no power. "The fool and his money are soon parted." Capital is only an instrument. It is effective only when it represents a single will in action. The decision of one man has greater force than the feeble or clashing desires of thousands.

It is not true that wealth is the result of "labor applied to the forces of nature." The gaining of wealth is the result of wise direction or of skillful manipulation. In the long run, the majority of employers of labor are eaten out of house and home by employees who have no stake in the result, and, therefore, nothing to lose from failure.

The little boy in the child's story* says:

"My feet, they haul me round the house;
    They hoist me up the stairs;
I only have to steer them, and
    They ride me everywheres."

The average man's view of capital is of the same kind. He underestimates the importance of the steering part of the work, without which no labor yields wealth, and without which capital is ineffective. If he understood the value of wise direction of effort he would cease to be an average man.

The industrial dangers which threaten our country come not primarily from the power of the rich, but from the weakness of the poor. Too often the poor are taking to themselves a leisure which they have never earned. The price they have paid in life is the price of poverty. If part of it goes for whisky and tobacco, the rest must go for rags and dirt. Even the lowest reward of labor well spent will buy a happy home. But, with-

---

*From "The Lark," San Francisco.

out frugality and temperance, no rate of wages and no division of profits can avail to save a man from poverty; and the waste of one man injures not only himself, but carries harm to all his neighbors, joined to him in disastrous industrial alliance.

We are told that "poverty is the relentless hell" that yawns beneath civil society, So it is; and a similar comparison may be made in the case of the penalty which follows the violation of any other law of ethics and economics. "By their long memories the gods are known." Under their laws we live, and beneath us forever yawn their penalties. But we may change this metaphor a little. May it not be that this yawning, "relentless hell," is due in part to the presence among us of the yawning, relentless horde of men who would gain something for nothing? In whatever form of industry this influence is felt, it must come as industrial depression.

The essential cause of poverty is the failure to adapt means to ends. A woman in the Tennessee mountains explained once the condition of the "poor whites" in these words: "Poor folks have poor ways." That their ways are poor is the cause of their economic weakness. And again it is written: "The destruction of the poor is their poverty." Without skill to bring about favorable results, the poor are constantly victims of circumstances. These conditions of their lives lead to reduced vitality, lowered morality, and loss of self-respect. Effective life demands, as Huxley tells us, "absolute veracity of thought and action." Those who lack this will always be poor, whatever our social or industrial conditions, unless they become slaves to the

will of others, or unless their weakness be placed as a
burden on collective effort. It is certainly true that,
even though each man in America were industrious
to the full measure of his powers, the poor would still
"be with us." There will always be impracticable and
incapable men, those who put forth effort enough, but
who can do nothing for others that others are likely
to value. There will still be the sick and the broken,
the weak and the unfortunate. But if these were our
only poor, all men would be their neighbors. Statistics have shown that, of ten persons in distress in our
great cities, the condition of six is due to intemper-
ance, idleness, or vice, three to old age and weakness
following a thriftless or improvident youth, and one to
sickness, accident, or loss of work. The unfortunate
poor are but a small fraction of the great pauperism.
Were there no pretenders, all who travel on the road to
Jericho should be Good Samaritans. Why not? The
impulse to charity is the common instinct of humanity;
but the priest and Levite of our day have been so many
times imposed upon that all distress is viewed with suspicion. The semblance of misfortune is put on for the
sake of the oil, and the wine, and the pieces of silver.
We "pass by on the other side" because in our times
we have learned that even common charity may become
a crime. We have seen the man who has "fallen by the
wayside" put vitriol in his children's eyes that their
distress may appeal to us yet more strongly. We have
learned that to give food to starving children thereby
helps to condemn them to a life of misery and crime.
To give something for nothing is to help destroy the
possibility of self-activity. And money gained without

effort is ill-gotten gain.   A blind man, to whom some
one offered money, once said: "We should never give
money to a blind man; for he needs all the strength he
can have to help him compete with men who can see."
Ill-timed help destroys the rationality of life.   If the
laws of life were changed so that the fool and his money
were less easily parted, money would be wasted still
more foolishly than now.

Money given outright is as dangerous as a gift of
opium, and its results are not altogether different.   Only
the very strong can receive it with safety.   Only the very
earnest can repay with interest the loans of the gods.
Unearned rewards cut the nerve of future effort.   The
man who receives a windfall forever after watches the
wind.   There is but one good fortune to the earnest man.
This is opportunity; and sooner or later opportunity will
come to him who can make use of it.   Undeserved help
brings the germs of idleness.   Even nature is too generous
for perfect justice.   She gives to vagabonds enough to
perpetuate vagabondage.

The strength of New England lay in this — that on
her rocky hills only the industrious man could make a
living, and with the years the habit of industry became
ingrained in the New England character.   This strength
to-day is seen wherever New England influences have
gone.   The great West was built with the savings of
New England.   Go to the prairies of Iowa, where the
earth gives her choicest bounty for the least effort, over
and over again you will find that these rich farms bear
mortgages given to some farmer on the Massachusetts
hills.   The poor land of the mountains, worked by a
man who gave his time and his work, yields enough to

pay for the rich land, too. The Iowa farmer must work with equal diligence if he is to hold his own against the competition of Massachusetts.

Not long ago, I crossed the State of Indiana on the railway train. It makes no difference where or in what direction. It was a bright day in April, when the sun shone on the damp earth, and when one could almost hear the growing of the grass. There are days and days like this, which every farm boy can remember — days which brought to him the delight of living; but to the thrifty farmer these days brought also their duties of plowing, and planting, and sowing. The hope of the spring was in all this work, and no one thought of it as drudgery. The days were all too short for the duties which crowded, and the right to rest could only come when the grain was in the ground, where the forces of nature might wake it into life. An hour in the growing spring is worth a week in the hot midsummer; and he must be a poor farmer, indeed, who does not realize this.

And I thought that day of the freedom of the farmer. He trades with nature through no middle-man. Nowhere is forethought and intelligence better paid than in dealings with Mother Nature. She is as honest as eternity, and she never fails to meet the just dues of all who have claims upon her. She returns some fifty-fold, some hundred-fold, for all that is intrusted to her; never fifty-fold to him who deserves a hundred.

Just then the train stopped for a moment at a flag-station — a village called Cloverdale, a name suggestive of sweet blossoms and agricultural prosperity. A commercial traveler, dealing in groceries and tobacco, got off; a

crate of live chickens was put on, and the cars started
again.   The stopping of a train was no rare event in
that village; for it happens two or three times every day.
The people had no welcome for the commercial traveler,
no tears were shed over the departure of the chickens;
yet on the station steps I counted forty men and boys
who were there when the train came in.   Farm boys,
who ought to have been at work in the fields; village
boys, who might have been doing something somewhere
— every interest of economics and æsthetics alike calling
them away from the station and off to the farms.

Two men attended to the business of the station.   The
solitary traveler went his own way.   The rest were there
because they had not the moral strength to go anywhere
else.   They were there on the station steps, dead to all
life and hope, with only force enough to stand around
and "gape."

At my destination I left the train, and going to the
hotel, I passed on a street corner the noisy vender of a
rheumatism cure.   Sixty men and boys who had no
need for cures of any kind— for they were already dead
— were standing around with mouths open and brains
shut, engaged in killing time.   I was sorry to see that
many of these were farmers.   All this time their neg-
lected farms lay bathed in the sunlight, the earth ready
to rejoice at the touch of a hoe.

Not long ago I had occasion to cross a village square.
I saw many busy men upon it, men who had a right to
be there, because they were there on their own business.
Each one takes part in the great task of caring for the
world when he is able and willing to care for himself.
On the corner of the square a wandering vagrant, with a

cracked accordion, set forth strains of doleful music. The people stood around him, like flies around a drop of molasses. An hour later I returned. The accordion and its victims were still there, as if chained to the spot. The birdlime of habitual idleness was on their feet, and they could not get away. They will never get away. The mark of doom is on them. They will stay there forever.

In these days, the farmer and the workingman have many grievances of which they did not know a generation ago. The newspapers and the stump-speakers tell us of these wrongs, and, from time to time, huge unions and alliances are formed to set them right. I go back to the old farm in Western New York on which I was born —the farm my father won from the forest, and on which he lived in freedom and independence, knowing no master, dreading no oppression. I find on that farm to-day tenants who barely make a living. I go over the farm; I see unpruned fruit trees, wasted forest trees, farm implements rusting in the rain and sun, falling gates, broken wagons, evidences of wasted time and unthrifty labor. When one sees such things, he must ask how much of the oppression of the farmer is the fault of the times and how much is the fault of the man.

It may be in part the poorness of his ways, rather than the aggression of his neighbors, which has plunged him into poverty. In very truth, it is both; but the one may be the cause of the other. It is only the born slave that can be kept in slavery. If a farmer spend a day in the harvest-time in efforts to send a fool to the Legislature, or a knave to Congress, should he complain if the laws the fools and knaves make add to his own taxes?

If he stand all day in the public square spellbound by
a tramp with an accordion; or, still worse, if he lounge
about on the sawdust floor of a saloon, talking the stuff
we agree to call politics, never reading a book, never
thinking a thought above the level of the sawdust floor,
need he be surprised if his opinions do not meet with
respect?

I can well remember the time when the farmer was
a busy man. There is many a farm to-day on which he
is still busy. It does not take a close observer to recognize these farms. You can tell them as far as you can
see. Their owners are in alliance with the forces of
nature. The gods are on their side, and they only ask
from politicians that they keep out of their sunlight.
Their butter sells for money; their oats are clean; their
horses are in demand; whatever they touch is genuine
and prosperous. The cattle call the farmer up at dawn;
the clover needs him in the morning; the apples and
potatoes in the afternoon; the corn must be husked at
night. A busy man the successful farmer is. Being
busy, he finds time for everything. He reads "bound
books"; he enjoys the pleasures of travel; he educates
his family; he keeps intelligent watch on the affairs of the
day. He does not find time to stand on the station steps
in the middle of the afternoon to watch a thousand trains
go by on a thousand consecutive days. He carries no
handicap load of tobacco and whisky. He goes to the
county-seat when he has business there. He goes with
clean clothes, and comes back with a clean conscience.
He has not time to spend each seventh day on the court-
house square talking the dregs of scandal and politics
with men whose highest civic conception is balanced by

a two-dollar bill; nor has he time to waste on nostrum-venders or vagrants with accordions.

I hear the farmers complaining — and most justly complaining — of high taxes; but no duty on iron was ever so great as the tax he pays who leaves his mowing-machine unsheltered in the storm. The tax on land is high; but he pays a higher tax who leaves his meadows to grow up to whiteweed and thistles. The tax for good roads is high; but a higher toll is paid by the farmer who goes each week to town in mud knee-deep to his horses. There is a high tax on personal property; but it is not so high as the tax on time which is paid by the man who spends his Saturdays loitering about the village streets, or playing games of chance in some " dead-fall " saloon.

Mowing-machines, thrashers, harvesters, and all the array of labor-saving contrivances of an altruistic age serve nothing if they are not rightly used. They are burdens, not helps, if the time they save be not taken in further production. Labor-saving machinery becomes the costliest of luxuries if the time it saves be turned into idleness or dissipation.

I know a hundred farmers in Southern Indiana who lose regularly one-sixth of their time by needless visits to the county-seat, and in making these visits needlessly long. The farmer's time is his capital; its use is his income. One-sixth of his time means one-sixth of his income, or else his whole time is not worth saving. It is this sixth which represents the difference between poverty and prosperity. If this wasted sixth were saved by every farmer in Indiana, the State would be an industrial paradise. To have lived in Indiana would be an education in itself. People would come from the ends of the earth to see the land which has solved the labor question.

But it may be that their own valuation is a just one. Perhaps there are some farmers whose time has no economic value. There are other such in every community and in every line in life. The idiot, the insane, the broken, the *dilettante*, the criminal. For some of these great hospitals are maintained, because they can be more cheaply supported in public lodgings at the common cost. Shall we add the weary farmer to this list? Why not have a great State hospital for all men whose time is worthless — a great square courtyard, covered with sawdust, with comfortable dry-goods boxes, where they might sit for the whole day, and the whole year, talking politics or "playing pedro" to the music of the hand-organ, watching the trains go by? The rest of the world could then go on with the world's work, with some addition, no doubt, to the taxes, but with corresponding gain in having the streets open, the saloons closed, the demagogue silenced, and the pastures free from weeds and thistles.

The frost is a great economic agent as a spur to human activity. There are lands where the frost never comes, and where not one-sixth, but six-sixths, of the time of almost every man is devoted to any purpose rather than that of attending to his own affairs. It is nature's great hospital for the incurably lazy. The motto of the tropics is summed up in one word, "Mañana," "to-morrow." To-morrow let us do it; we must eat and sleep to-day. "Mañana por la mañana," one hears over and over again at every suggestion involving the slightest effort.

It is too warm to-day; the sunshine is too bright; the shade too pleasant; —"Mañana" let it be. This is the land where nothing is ever done. "Why should we do things when to rest and not to do is so much pleasanter? There is the endless succession of to-morrows. They have come on to us since eternity, and surely they will continue to come. Let us rest in the shade, and wait for the next to-morrow."

I have not meant that one word of this should be a special criticism of the American farmer. It is still broadly true that the farmers as a class are the sanest of our people, the least infected by follies and with most faith in the natural relations of cause and effect. The farmers have not yet come to feel that their advancement must be assured through the repression of others. They have not yet turned from nature to legislation in their search for wealth. The farmer deals with the earth directly. It is the earth, not society, that owes him a living. Of all callings, his is least related to the conventionalities of man. That he has scorned these conventionalities, that he has "hated the narrow town and all its fashions," has been the source of some of his misfortunes. For the town is nearer the center of legislation, and it has not been slow to cast burdens upon others for its own purposes. But if the farmer is the victim of unequal taxation or of unjust discriminations, as he certainly is, it is his duty and his privilege to make matters right. Even though sometimes he acts blindly —with the discrimination of the "bull in a china-shop," —as when he votes for bad roads, cheap men, cheap money, and crippled public schools, it is not a source of discouragement. Men in cities do even worse than this.   The farmer will know better when he has looked more deeply into the matter.   But whatever the repeal of bad legislation may do, the primal necessity remains.

> " He who by the plow would thrive,
>   Himself must either hold or drive."

Whoever will prosper in any line of life must save his own time and do his own thinking.   He must spend neither time nor money which he has not earned.   He must not do in a poor way what others do in a better. The change of worse men for better is always painful — it is often cruel.   But it must come.   The remedy is to make men better, so that there need be no change.

The rise of the common man which has been going on all these centuries demands that the common man must rise.   This is the "change from status to contract," to use the words of Sir Henry Mayne, which is the essential fact in modern progress.   But this rise has its sorrows as well as its joys.   Man cannot use the powers and privileges of civilization without sharing its responsibilities.

In the progress of civilization every form of labor must tend to become a profession.   The brain must control the hand.   The advance of civilization means the dominance of brain.   It means the elimination of unskilled work.   The man who does not know, nor care to know, how farming is carried on, cannot remain a farmer.   Whatever human laws may do, the laws of the gods will not leave him long in possession of the ground. If he does not know his business, he must let go of the earth, which will be taken by some one who does.   In the words of a successful farmer whom I know, "Let other people's affairs alone, mind your own business, and you will have prosperity." If not in the fullest measure, it will still be all that you have paid for, and thus all that you deserve.

I have wished to teach a single lesson, true alike to all men,— the lesson of the saving of time.

To you, as students, I may say: The pathway of your lives lies along the borders of the Land of Mañana. It is easy to turn into it and to lose yourselves among its palms and bananas. That thus far in your lives you are still on the right way is shown by your presence here to-day. Were it not so, you would be here to-morrow. You would wait for your education till the day that never comes.

Different men have different powers. To come to the full measure of these powers, constitutes success in life. But power is only relative. It depends on the factor of time. With time enough, we could, any of us, do anything. With this great multiplier, it matters little what the other factor is. Any man would be all men, could he have time enough. With time enough, all things would be possible. With eternity, man becomes as the gods. But our time on earth is not eternity. We can do but little at the most. And the grim humorist reminds us "we shall be a long time dead." So every hour we waste carries away its life, as the drop of falling water carries away the rock. Every lost day takes away its cubit from our stature.

So let us work while yet it is day, and when the evening falls we may rest under the shade of the palm-trees. He who has been active has earned the right to sleep; and when we have finished our appointed work, "the

R

rest is silence." The toilsome, busy earth on which the strength of our lives has been spent shall be taken away from us. It shall be "rolled away like a scroll," giving place to that eternity which has no limit, nor environment, and whose glory is past all understanding.

XVII.

THE NEW UNIVERSITY.*

WE come together to-day for the first time as teachers and students. With this relation the life of the Leland Stanford Junior University begins. It is such personal contact of young men and young women with scholars and investigators which constitutes the life of the university. It is for us as teachers and students in the university's first year to lay the foundations of a school which may last as long as human civilization. Ours is the youngest of the universities, but it is heir to the wisdom of all the ages, and with this inheritance it has the promise of a rapid and sturdy growth.

Our university has no history to fall back upon; no memories of great teachers haunt its corridors; in none of its rooms appear the traces which show where a great man has lived or worked. No tender associations cling, ivy-like, to its fresh, new walls. It is hallowed by no traditions. It is hampered by none. Its finger-posts still point forward. Traditions and associations it is ours to make. From our work the future of the university will grow, as the splendid lily from the modest bulb.

But the future, with its glories and its responsibilities, will be in other hands. It is ours at the beginning to give the University its form, its tendencies, its customs. The power of precedent will cause to be repeated over

* President's Address, Opening Day of the Leland Stanford Junior University, October 1, 1891.

and over again everything that we do — our errors as well as our wisdom. It becomes us, then, to begin the work modestly, as under the eye of the coming ages. We must lay the foundations broad and firm, so as to give full support to whatever edifice the future may build. Ours is the humbler task, but not the least in importance, and our work will not be in vain if all that we do is done in sincerity. As sound as the rocks from which these walls are hewn should be the work of every teacher who comes within them. To the extent that this is true will the university be successful. Unless its work be thus "wrought in a sad sincerity," nothing can redeem it from failure. In this feeling, and realizing, too, that only the help we give to the men and women whose lives we reach can justify our presence here, we are ready to begin our work.

We hope to give to our students the priceless legacy of the educated man, the power of knowing what really is. The higher education should bring men into direct contact with truth. It should help to free them from the dead hands of old traditions and to enable them to form opinions worthy of the new evidence each new day brings before them. An educated man should not be the slave of the past, not a copy of men who have gone before him. He must be in some degree the founder of a new intellectual dynasty; for each new thinker is a new type of man. Whatever is true is the truest thing in the universe, and mental and moral strength alike come from our contact with it.

Every influence which goes out from these halls should emphasize the value of truth. The essence of scholarship is to know something which is absolutely true; to have, in the words of Huxley, "some knowledge to the certainty of which no authority could add nor take away one jot nor tittle, and to which the tradition of a thousand years is but as the hearsay of yesterday." The scholar, as was once said of our great chemist, Benjamin Silliman, must have "faith in truth as truth, faith that there is a power in the universe good enough to make truth-telling safe, and strong enough to make truth-telling effective." The personal influence of genuineness, as embodied in the life of a teacher, is one of the strongest moral forces which the school can bring to its aid; for moral training comes not mainly by precept, but by practice. We may teach the value of truth to our students by showing that we value it ourselves.

In like manner, the value of right living can be taught by right examples. In the words of a wise teacher,* "Science knows no source of life but life. The teacher is one of the accredited delegates of civilization. In Heine's phrase, he is a Knight of the Holy Ghost. If virtue and integrity are to be propagated, they must be propagated by people who possess them. If this child-world about us that we know and love is to grow up into righteous manhood and womanhood, it must have a chance to see how righteousness looks when it is lived. That this may be so, what task have we but to garrison our State with men and women? If we can do that, if we can have in every square mile in our country a man or woman whose total influence is a civilizing power, we shall get from our educational system all it can give and all that we can desire." So we may hope that this new school will do its part in the work of civilization, side by

* Professor William Lowe Bryan.

side with her elder sister, the University of the State, and in perfect harmony with every agency which makes for right thinking and right living.   The harvest is bounteous, but laborers are still all too few; for a generous education should be the birthright of every man and woman in America.

I shall not try to-day to give you our ideal of what a university should be.   If our work is successful, our ideals will appear in the daily life of the school.   In a school, as in a fortress, it is not the form of the building, but the strength of the materials, which determine its effectiveness.   With a garrison of hearts of oak, it may not matter even whether there be a fortress.   Whatever its form, or its organization, or its pretensions, the character of the university is fixed by the men who teach. "Have a university in shanties, nay in tents," Cardinal Newman has said, "but have great teachers in it."   The university spirit flows out from these teachers, and its organization serves mainly to bring them together. "Colleges can only serve us," says Emerson, "when their aim is not to drill, but to create ; when they gather from far every ray of various genius to their hospitable halls, and by their concentrated fires set the heart of their youth in flame."   Strong men make universities strong.   A great man never fails to leave a great mark on every youth with whom he comes in contact.   Too much emphasis cannot be laid on this: that the real purpose of the university organization is to produce a university atmosphere—such an atmosphere as gathered itself around Arnold at Rugby, around Döllinger at Munich, around Linnæus at Upsala, around Werner at Freiburg, around Agassiz at Cambridge, around Mark Hopkins at Williamstown, around Andrew D. White at Ithaca, around all great teachers everywhere.

A professor to whom original investigation is unknown should have no place in a university. Men of commonplace or second-hand scholarship are of necessity men of low ideals, however much the fact may be disguised. A man of high ideals must be an investigator. He must know and think for himself. Only such as do this can be really great as teachers. Some day our universities will recognize that their most important professors may be men who teach no classes, devoting their time and strength wholly to advanced research. Their presence and example will be, perhaps, worth to the student body a hundred-fold more than the precepts and drill of the others. They set high standards of thought. They help to create the university spirit, without which any college is but a grammar school of a little higher pretensions.

And above and beyond all learning is the influence of character, the impulse to virtue and piety which comes from men whose lives show that virtue and piety really exist. For the life of the most exalted as well as the humblest of men, there can be nobler motto than that inscribed by the great scholar of the last century over his home at Hammarby : " *Innocue vivito; numen adest.*" Live blameless; God is near. "This," said Linnæus, "is the wisdom of my life." Every advance which we make toward the realization of the truth of the permanence and immanence of law, brings us nearer to Him who is the great First Cause of all law and all phenomena.

While the work of the teachers must make the kernel

of the university, we must rejoice that here at Palo Alto
even the husks are beautiful.   Beauty and fitness are
great forces in education.   Every object with which the
young mind comes in contact leaves on it its trace.
"Nothing is unimportant in the life of man," and the
least feature of our surroundings has its influence, greater
or less.   "There was a child went forth every day,"
Walt Whitman tells us, "and the first object that it
looked upon, that object it became."   It may be for
a moment or an hour, or "for changing cycles of years."
The essence of civilization is exposure to refining and
humanizing influences.   "A dollar in a university,"
Emerson tells us, "is worth more than a dollar in a
jail," and every dollar spent in making a university
beautiful will be repaid with interest in the enriching of
the students' lives.

It has been a reproach of America that for the best
of her sons and daughters she has done the least.   She
has built palaces for lunatics, idiots, crippled, and blind,
— nay, even for criminals and paupers.   But the college
students— "the young men of sound mind and earnest
purpose, the noblest treasures of the State," to quote
the words of President White, "she has housed in vile
barracks."   The student has no need for luxury.   Plain
living has ever gone with high thinking.   But grace
and fitness have an educative power too often forgotten
in this utilitarian age.   These long corridors with their
stately arches, these circles of waving palms, will have
their part in the students' training as surely as the chemical laboratory or the seminary-room.   Each stone in
the quadrangle shall teach its lesson of grace and of
genuineness, and this Valley of Santa Clara — the valley

of "holy clearness" — shall occupy a warm place in every student's heart. Pictures of this fair region will cling to his memory amid the figures of draughting-room. He will not forget the fine waves of our two mountain ranges, overarched by a soft blue Grecian sky, nor the ancient oak-trees, nor the gently sloping fields, changing from vivid green to richest yellow, as the seasons change. The noble pillars of the gallery of art, its rich treasures, the choicest remains of the ideals of past ages — all these, and a hundred other things which each one will find out for himself, shall fill his mind with bright pictures, never to be rubbed out in the wear of life. Thus in the character of every student shall be left some imperishable trace of the beauty of Palo Alto.

Agassiz once said: "The physical suffering of humanity, the wants of the poor, the craving of the hungry and naked, appeal to the sympathies of every one who has a human heart. But there are necessities which only the destitute student knows. There is a hunger and thirst which only the highest charity can understand and relieve; and on this solemn occasion let me say that every dollar given for higher education, in whatever department of knowledge, is likely to have a greater influence on the future character of our nation than even the thousands, hundred thousands, and millions which we have spent, or are spending, to raise the many to material ease and comfort."

I need not recall to you the history of the foundation of the Leland Stanford Junior University. It has its origin in the shadow of a great sorrow, and its purpose in the wish to satisfy for the coming generations the hunger and thirst after knowledge — that undying curiosity which is the best gift of God to man.   The influence of the boy, to the nobility of whose short life the Leland Stanford Junior University is a tribute and a remembrance, will never be lost in our country.   To him we owe the inspiration which led the founders to devote the earnings of the successful ventures of a busy life to the work of higher education.

Six years ago, in one of our California journals,* these words were used with reference to the work which we begin to-day: "Greater than the achievement of lasting honor among one's fellow-men of later generations, is it to become a living power among them forever.   It rarely happens to one man and woman to have both the power and the skill to thus live after death, working and shaping beneficently in the lives of many — not of tens nor of hundreds, but of thousands and of tens of thousands, as the generations follow on.   Herein is the wisdom of money spent in education, that each recipient of influence becomes in his time a center to transmit the same in every direction, so that it multiplies forever in geometric ratio.   This power to mold unborn generations for good, to keep one's hands mightily on human affairs after the flesh has been dust for years, seems not only more than mortal, but more than man.   Thus does man become co-worker with God in the shaping of the world to a good outcome."

The Golden Age of California begins when its gold is used for purposes like this.   From such deeds must rise the new California of the the coming century, no longer the California of the gold-seeker and the adventurer, but the abode of high-minded men and women, trained in

---

* Milicent W. Shinn, in The Overland Monthly.

the wisdom of the ages, and imbued with the love of nature, the love of man, and the love of God. And bright indeed will be the future of our State if, in the usefulness of the university, every hope and prayer of the founders shall be realized.